T0225773

PrestaShop Recipes

A Problem-Solution Approach

Arnaldo Pérez Castaño

Apress®

PrestaShop Recipes: A Problem-Solution Approach

Arnaldo Pérez Castaño
Havana, Cuba

ISBN-13 (pbk): 978-1-4842-2573-8   ISBN-13 (electronic): 978-1-4842-2574-5
DOI 10.1007/978-1-4842-2574-5

Library of Congress Control Number: 2017934221

Managing Director: Welmoed Spahr
Editorial Director: Todd Green
Acquisitions Editor: Louise Corrigan
Development Editor: James Markham
Technical Reviewer: Massimo Nardone
Coordinating Editor: Nancy Chen
Copy Editor: Ann Dickson
Compositor: SPi Global
Indexer: SPi Global
Artist: SPi Global
Cover image designed by Freepik

Distributed to the book trade worldwide by Springer Science+Business Media New York, 233 Spring Street, 6th Floor, New York, NY 10013. Phone 1-800-SPRINGER, fax (201) 348-4505, e-mail orders-ny@springer-sbm.com, or visit www.springeronline.com. Apress Media, LLC is a California LLC and the sole member (owner) is Springer Science + Business Media Finance Inc (SSBM Finance Inc). SSBM Finance Inc is a **Delaware** corporation.

For information on translations, please e-mail rights@apress.com, or visit http://www.apress.com/rights-permissions.

Apress titles may be purchased in bulk for academic, corporate, or promotional use. eBook versions and licenses are also available for most titles. For more information, reference our Print and eBook Bulk Sales web page at http://www.apress.com/bulk-sales.

Any source code or other supplementary material referenced by the author in this book is available to readers on GitHub via the book's product page, located at www.apress.com/9781484225738. For more detailed information, please visit http://www.apress.com/source-code.

Printed on acid-free paper

To my mother, my father, my family, and friends; thanks for being there for me.

Contents at a Glance

Contents

About the Author

Arnaldo Pérez Castaño is a computer scientist based in Cuba. He's the author of a series of programming books—*JavaScript Fácil*, *HTML y CSS Fácil*, and Python *Fácil* (Marcombo S.A.)—and writes for *MSDN Magazine*, VisualStudioMagazine.com, and *Smashing Magazine*. He is one of the co-founders of Havana Digital Enterprises and the creator of their first websites, www.havanaclassiccartour.com and www.havanadanceclass.com. His expertise includes Visual Basic, C#, .NET Framework, and artificial intelligence. He offers his services through freelancer.com. Cinema and music are two of his passions.

About the Technical Reviewer

Massimo Nardone has more than 22 years of experiences in security and web/mobile development, cloud computing, and IT architecture. His true IT passions are security and Android. He has been programming and teaching how to program with Android, Perl, PHP, Java, VB, Python, C/C++, and MySQL for more than 20 years.

He holds a Master of Science degree in computing science from the University of Salerno, Italy.

He has worked as a project manager, software engineer, research engineer, chief security architect, information security manager, PCI/SCADA auditor, and senior lead IT security/cloud/SCADA architect for many years. His technical skills include security, Android, cloud computing, Java, MySQL, Drupal, Cobol, Perl, web and mobile development, MongoDB, D3, Joomla, Couchbase, C/C++, WebGL, Python, Pro Rails, Django CMS, Jekyll, and Scratch.

He currently works as chief information security office (CISO) for CargotecOyj.

He worked as visiting lecturer and supervisor for exercises at the networking laboratory of the Helsinki University of Technology (Aalto University). He holds four international patents (PKI, SIP, SAML, and Proxy areas).

Massimo has reviewed more than 40 IT books for different publishing company and he is the co-author of *Pro Android Games* (Apress, 2015).

Introduction

This book is intended for all PrestaShop (PS) users and developers who would like to acquire a better understanding of this amazing content management system (CMS). It contains easy-to-follow recipes that will help you achieve various customizations on your website in simple, clear steps. These recipes will not only aid you in solving specific problems, but they will also provide you with the necessary tools and knowledge to develop any similar customization that's not included in the book.

Chapter 1 presents different recipes for showing you how to install and configure your PrestaShop website. Chapter 2 introduces the interesting topic of modules—the best alternative for providing extensibility and inject modified behavior into the system. Chapter 3 is a large chapter that demonstrates how to solve many front-end issues that you may come across someday. Chapter 4 explains how to find solutions for many of the problems related to core files of the CMS; those files are the classes and controllers. Chapters 5 and 6 are unique and extremely interesting chapters that will show you how to transform PS into a booking system and an events-based system. Chapter 7 treats the topic of SEO in PrestaShop and finally, Chapter 8, the simplest of all, explains how to solve maintenance-related problems.

The possibilities with this CMS are infinite and, by reading this book, you'll see that converting PS into a booking or events-based system is not the last frontier; much more can be achieved if the CMS is properly studied.

CHAPTER 1

■ ■ ■

Installation and Configuration

Since its creation in 2005, PrestaShop (PS) has been evolving into one of the most competitive e-commerce solutions ever conceived. Nowadays there are over 250,000 online stores powered by this amazing Content Management System (CMS), and the number keeps on growing. What is it that makes PS so attractive and applicable to start online businesses for people all around the world? To start answering this question, we may visit http://demo.prestashop.com/, a URL devoted for users who want to try this incredible CMS without any need to install it. Also, the purpose of this chapter will be to answer the previous question by demonstrating the following:

- How easy it is to install PS

- How to set your own local server for PS

- How to change your domain name by modifying database entries

- How to back up and restore your database

- How to migrate PS from one server to another

- How to enable SSL in your local server

- How to enable SSL in PrestaShop

- How to share customers in a network of PS websites

- How to sell services instead of tangible products

- How to disable shipping

■ **Note** The shop configuration information can be found in the PrestaShop back panel following the path `Advanced Parameters -> Configuration Information`. There you can get a glance of server, database, and store information. In the near future, the latest PHP version supported by PrestaShop will be 5.4; therefore, it would be advisable to make sure your server is running under an equal or higher version.

© Arnaldo Pérez Castaño 2017
A. P. Castaño, *PrestaShop Recipes*, DOI 10.1007/978-1-4842-2574-5_1

1

1-1. Installing PrestaShop

Problem

You want to install PrestaShop in your server.

Solution

Installing PrestaShop can be extremely easy if you are using the appropriate hosting service. I personally recommend hosting on www.godaddy.com. I've hosted web applications with them before, and their server is exceptionally well optimized. Also, they have a CPanel with several tools for managing (for example, cloning) your websites as well as the possibility to install various CMSs on a given domain, which includes PrestaShop. Their installation process is very simple; some steps are hidden from customers and automatically handled by GoDaddy's machinery. This would be solution number one if you were looking for alternatives to install PS; of course, the decision ultimately depends on your conditions.

Solution number two would be to leave the entire installation process on your shoulders.

How It Works

Following the second alternative, we'd need to start by downloading the official PrestaShop package (www.prestashop.com/en/download). The result should be a .zip containing all PS files as shown in Figure 1-1.

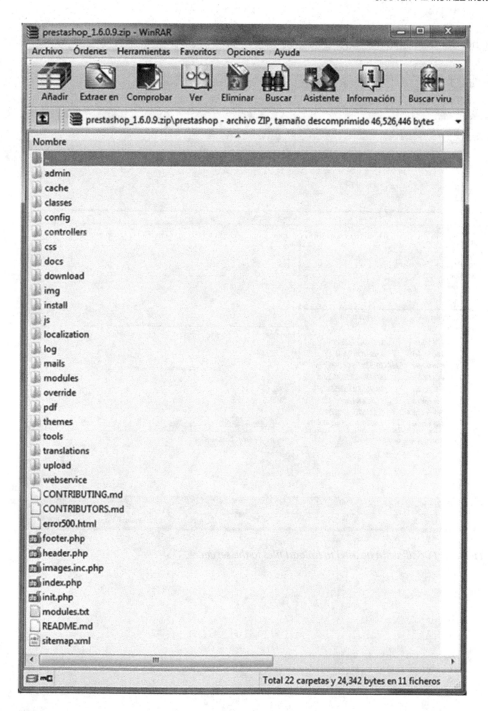

Figure 1-1. *PrestaShop package in .zip file*

Using an FTP client like FileZilla (Figure 1-2), we can upload or move the contents from the PS .zip to the folder that matches our domain in the server.

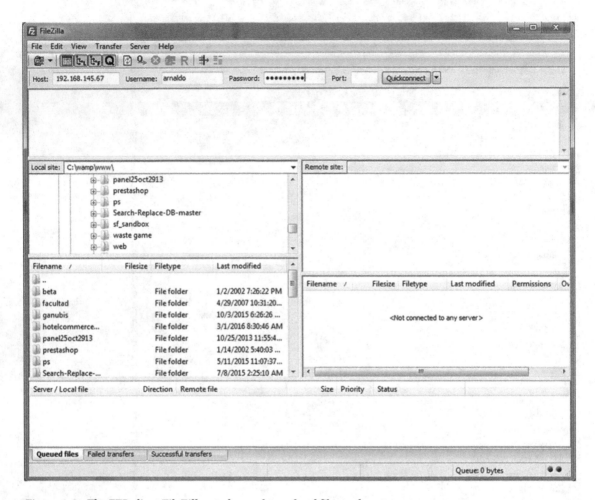

Figure 1-2. *The FTP client FileZilla can be used to upload files to the server.*

After uploading all files and having accessed our shop's URL, we can start the PrestaShop installation process, which consists of six steps as shown in Figure 1-3.

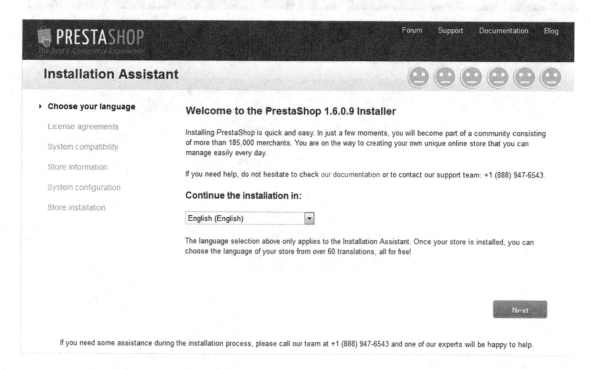

Figure 1-3. *PrestaShop installation page*

Steps 1–4 are form pages requesting basic information to initiate your online business. Therefore, we will skip them and move on to Step 5 in Figure 1-4, where we need to fill in details regarding our database.

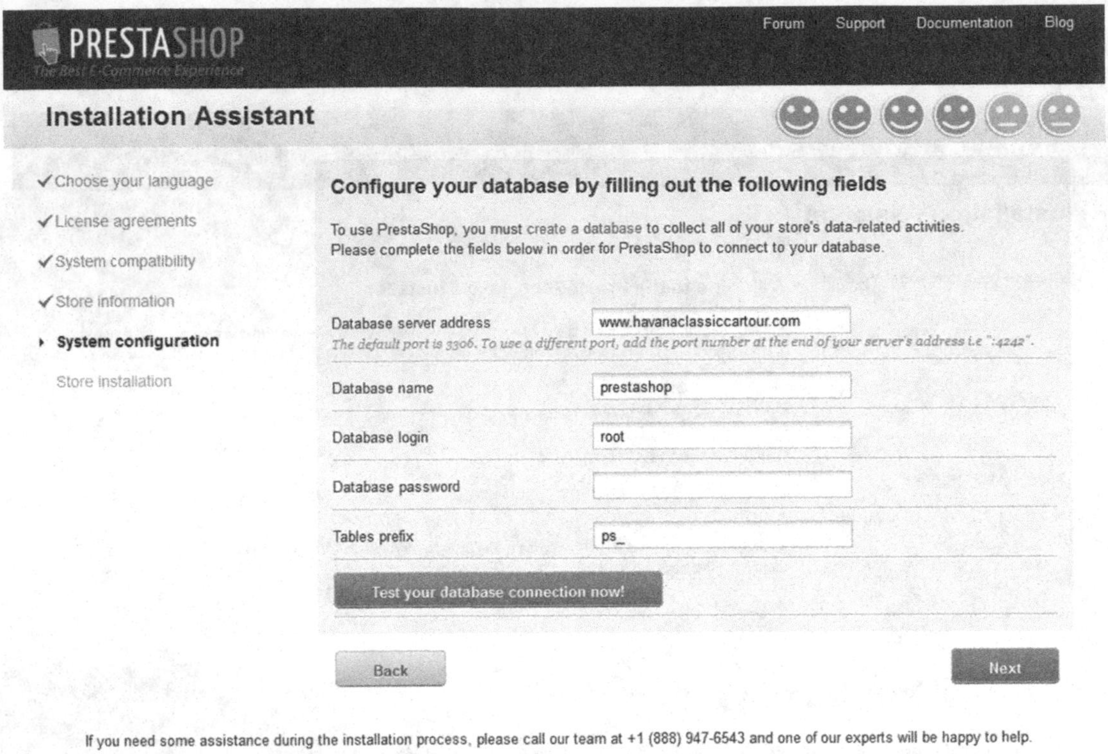

Figure 1-4. *Database details*

Every CMS requires a database to operate (save customer information, orders, products, and so on). We must indicate our database during PS installation; its creation could be handled in two different ways:

1. Through the MySQL command line

2. Using phpMyAdmin, a web interface for managing databases, which acts as a middle layer and ultimately operates on the MySQL command line level

In the first scenario, assuming MySQL is installed, we will be dealing with SQL statements, syntax, and a MySQL console similar to the one shown in the Figure 1-5.

```
Enter password:
Welcome to the MySQL monitor.   Commands end with ; or \g.
Your MySQL connection id is 4
Server version: 5.5.16-log MySQL Community Server (GPL)

Copyright (c) 2000, 2011, Oracle and/or its affiliates. All rights reserved.

Oracle is a registered trademark of Oracle Corporation and/or its
affiliates. Other names may be trademarks of their respective
owners.

Type 'help;' or '\h' for help. Type '\c' to clear the current input statement.

mysql>
```

Figure 1-5. *MySQL console*

To create a database, we simply type the command "create database *db_name*" where *db_name* is the name we want to give to our database, as shown in Figure 1-6.

```
mysql> create database prestashop;
Query OK, 1 row affected (0.00 sec)
```

Figure 1-6. *Database creation command*

To delete a database, we use the command "drop database *db_name*" where again *db_name* is the name of our database.

■ **Note**   Every command defined in the MySQL console should end with a semicolon (;) or \g. If you press Enter without having typed one of the previous symbols, you'll get into a multiline statement.

The second alternative is to use phpMyAdmin, available in most hosting services as seen in Figure 1-7.

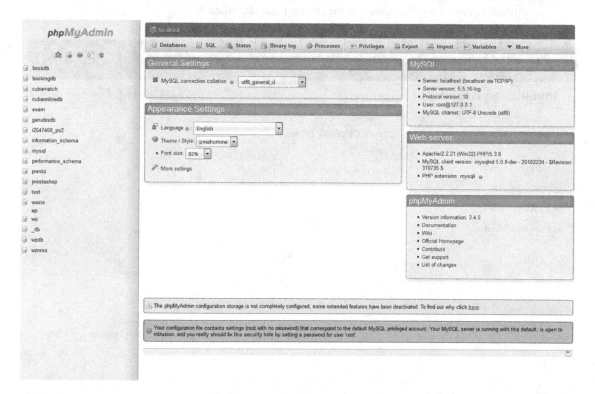

Figure 1-7. *phpMyAdmin home panel*

To create a database, we go to the Databases tab on the top menu, type the name we want to give our database in the Create New Database field, and click the Create button (Figure 1-8).

Figure 1-8. *Creating database in phpMyAdmin*

Once the database has been created, either by applying alternative one or two, the next step is to complete the System Configuration form on the installation page. The Database login and Database password fields are usually provided by your hosting service. If these are unknown at the moment, contact their support team. If you are using a local server, your login should be "root" and the password the empty string.

In a concluding step shown in Figure 1-9, the store is finally installed.

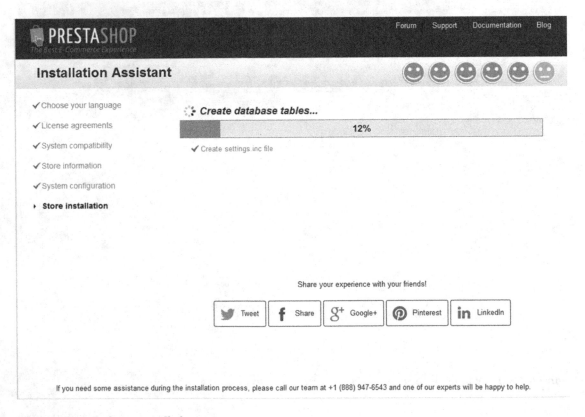

Figure 1-9. *Store being installed*

Now you can access the Front and Back ends. To access the PS Back Office, you need to delete the install folder that remains in the package folder. Afterward, it will be accessible providing the user/password combination specified during the installation process.

■ **Note** The Back Office URL is always determined by a folder whose name is given when the PS installation has been completed. If the folder name is admin1234, then you can access the Back Office through the URL www.mydomain.com/admin1234. This folder contains all code files for the administration sections (Figure 1-10).

Figure 1-10. Back Office entry point

Now the store is visible when someone types the URL on the browser and the installation process has been completed. It's time to start perusing the Back Office and creating, deleting, updating your products, categories, and so on.

1-2. Installing Your Local Server for PS

Problem

You want to install a server in your PC to manage, develop, test, customize your store, or simply try PrestaShop without the need to pay for a hosting service.

Solution

To understand the features that we'll demand from the server, we must first examine PrestaShop requirements.

PS was developed using PHP as programming language in its pure form, and it follows a three-layer architecture that resembles the MVC (Model View Controller) design pattern. PS developers decided not to use any PHP framework so as to obtain the highest performance and code legibility. Some of its most important features are the following.

- It is easy to install.
- User interface is relatively friendly.
- It supports features such as e-mail follow-up automation, SEO, and so on.
- It has high flexibility in configuration.

The web server commonly used for interacting with PHP dynamic pages is Apache, without any doubt the most popular and successful web server in the market for the last 20 years. Apache has a modular architecture; its modules provide extended functionality that you can activate or deactivate at will. The `mod_rewrite` module, for instance, is generally applied to convert dynamic PHP pages into static HTML pages seeking to hide the code from visitors and search engines.

The Database Management System (DBMS) used is MySQL, the relational, multithread, multiuser system with the top number of web installations these days. Companies like Amazon, Craigslist, NASA, and Google all use MySQL. Many developers choose it because it's simple and decently powerful; thus, the balance between simplicity and power in MySQL is almost perfect for the Web.

Fortunately for us, several web infrastructures have been created that encompass all of the previous technologies in one single global solution, among these it would be worth mentioning the following:

1. XAMPP (X = any operating System, A = Apache, M = MySQL, PP = PHP and Perl)

2. LAMP (L = Linux, A = Apache, M = MySQL, P = PHP)

3. MAMP (M = Mac, A = Apache, M = MySQL, P = PHP)

4. WAMP (W = Windows, A = Apache, M = MySQL, P = PHP)

WAMP, for example, can be installed in any PC running Microsoft Windows; it incorporates Apache as web server, MySQL as DBMS, and PHP as programming language. It also includes phpMyAdmin.

How It Works

The WAMP solution is actually a medium-size server. It comes with the basic modules and extensions that we need to execute our web applications. It's not a giant, but it will do perfectly for our purpose.

■ **Note**   WAMP can be downloaded from its official page, `www.wampserver.com`.

To install WAMP, we simply click the executable (.exe), the one we should get after download (Figure 1-11).

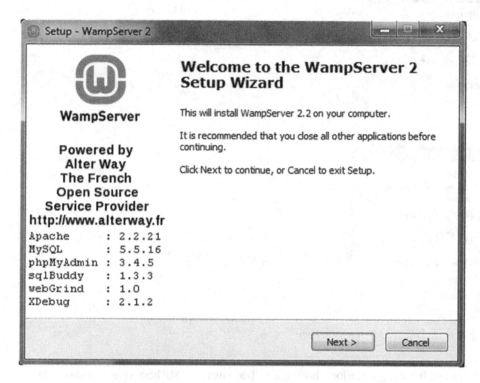

Figure 1-11. *WAMP server setup*

The version we are installing is packed not only with phpMyAdmin, but also with SqlBuddy, WebGrind, and XDebug. The last one is a PHP extension that allows for code debugging.

Once the setup has been completed, we'll be able to see an icon on the task bar representing a daemon process from WAMP. After clicking on that icon, a dialog should pop up (Figure 1-12).

Figure 1-12. *Dialog after clicking WAMP daemon icon*

Starting all services and browsing to the local host URL will take us to WAMP home page, as shown in Figure 1-13.

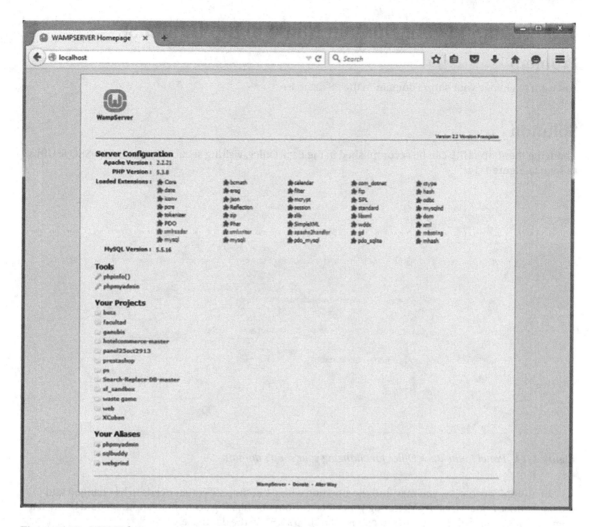

Figure 1-13. *WAMP home page*

Note that WAMP presents us a list of all web applications under path/www, where path is a folder specified during installation by default C:/wamp.

The www folder is the place where we need to copy and paste the PrestaShop package and, in general, any folder containing a website that we wish to include in our server. After copying the package, a link with the name of its folder should appear on the previous list. If we click this link, we'll be taken to the shop.

■ **Note**   If WAMP starts all services correctly, the daemon icon turns green 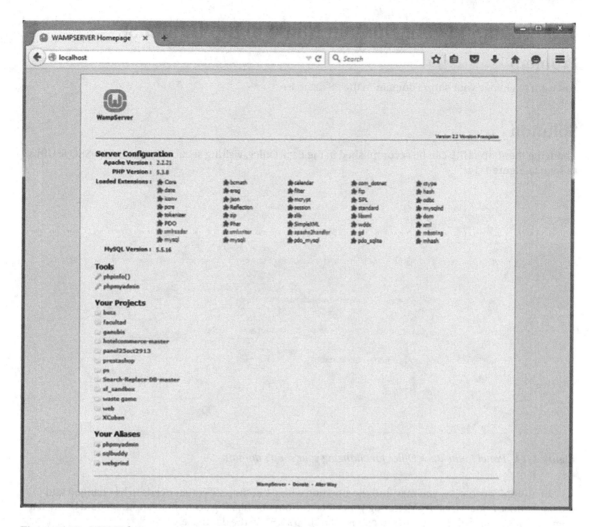. If there's an error, the daemon will display yellow or red; in that case, check that each service is running. Apache, for instance, might not be running because the port on which it is supposed to start may be occupied by another process. Therefore, you'd need to edit the http.conf file and change its port.

1-3. Changing Your Domain Name in the Database

Problem

You want to change your shop's domain in the PS database.

Solution

Changing the shop's URL can be accomplished in the Back Office, visiting section Preferences->SEO & URLs, as seen in Figure 1-14.

Figure 1-14. *Panel in the Back Office for changing your shop's domain*

In multiple scenarios, you may find the situation where the shop's domain needs to be changed and the Back Office is inaccessible. Migrating your website from one hosting account to another could be such a scenario. In this case, the solution is to change the shop's URL in the database.

How It Works

Let's assume we have installed PS in our local server and it's running under localhost/prestashop (Figure 1-15). By modifying entries in the database, we'll change it from localhost/prestashop to localhost:8181/prestashop. These entries we'll be altered using phpMyAdmin.

Figure 1-15. *PS running at localhost*

In phpMyAdmin home page, let's find the Databases section on the top menu and eventually select our PS database, as shown in Figure 1-16.

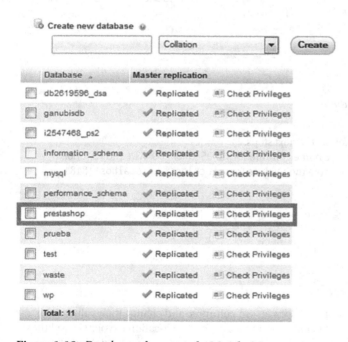

Figure 1-16. *Databases shown at phpMyAdmin*

■ **Note**   In case you don't know what database PS was using, the information can be found by opening the file config/ settings.inc.php with any text editor and locating the line define('_DB_NAME_', X). In this case, X should be the name of your PS database.

Once you clicked your database, a new page will display giving detailed information on PS tables (Figure 1-17).

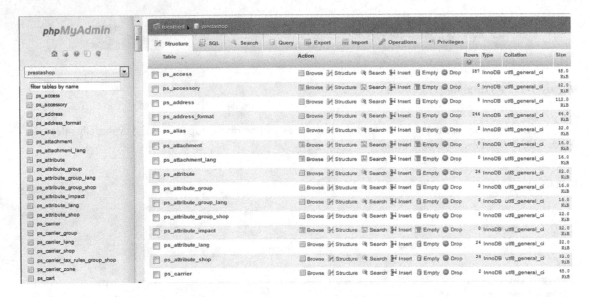

Figure 1-17. *PS tables displayed at phpMyAdmin*

Now, to change our shop's domain, we follow the next steps.

Find the ps_configuration table and in the name column, locate PS_SHOP_DOMAIN and PS_SHOP_DOMAIN_SSL (Figure 1-18). Edit both entries, altering their values from localhost to localhost:8181.

NULL	PS_SHOP_DOMAIN	localhost
NULL	PS_SHOP_DOMAIN_SSL	localhost

Figure 1-18. *PS variables to modify*

Find the ps_shop_url table and edit the domain, domain_ssl columns, and change their values from localhost to localhost:8181. The physical_uri column defines the physical location of your shop within the server. For instance, if your domain is www.havanaclassiccartour.com and your website is located inside a folder named prestashop in the entry point to your domain, then you will access your shop from www.havanaclassiccartour.com/prestashop, thus, in that case, physical_uri = /prestashop.

Since we are doing all of these changes in our local server, we also need to edit the Apache http.conf file to modify the server's domain. Edit that file and locate the line ServerName 127.0.0.1 and modify it to ServerName 127.0.0.1:8181. Now we can access our shop from the new domain as seen in Figure 1-19.

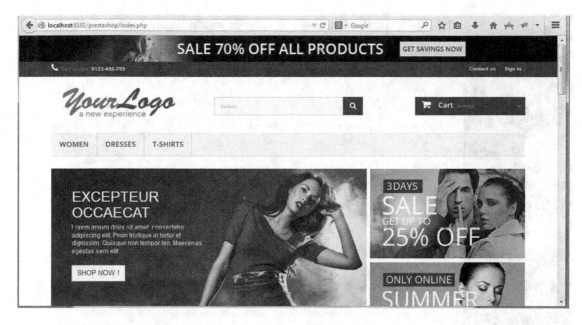

Figure 1-19. *Shop's domain modified*

Finally, we solved the problem assuming the shop was installed on a local server and accessible via localhost (127.0.0.1). This strategy is easily translatable to a shop with a real domain by simply exchanging localhost with your domain (www.yourdomain.com) in the previous pages.

1-4. Backing Up and Restoring Your Database

Problem

You want to back up your PrestaShop database to prevent information losses, to migrate your website, and so on. Eventually, you also want to restore your database from that backup.

Solution

To back up your database, you have two alternatives; you can do it via the PS Back Office or with phpMyAdmin.

How It Works

If you visit the Back Office and go to Advanced Parameters->DB Backup, you'll find the PS tool for backing up your database (Figure 1-20).

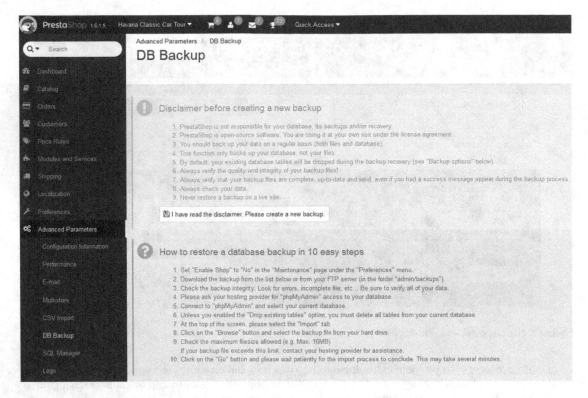

Figure 1-20. *Database backup*

The backup consists of a `.gz` compressing an `.sql` file that contains all SQL statements to recreate the database.

The second alternative would be to use phpMyAdmin directly, selecting the database we want and going to the Export tab as shown in Figure 1-21.

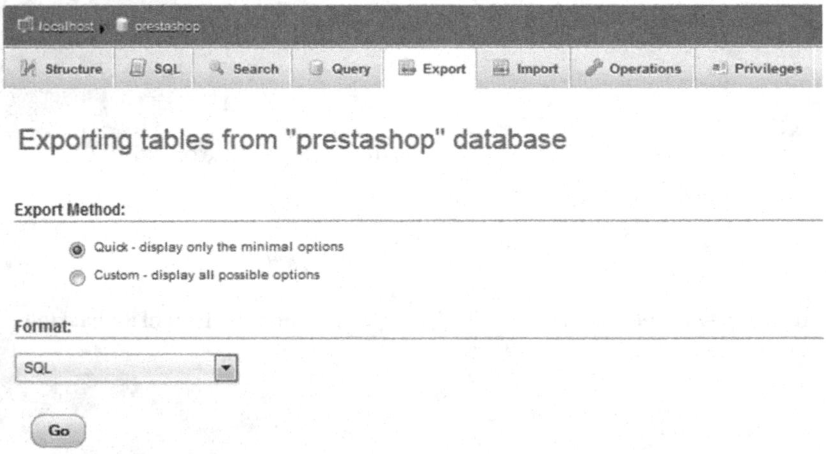

Figure 1-21. *Exporting database in phpMyAdmin*

Following this approach, we would need to select the desired format (usually `.sql`) and click Go. Button (Figure 1-22).

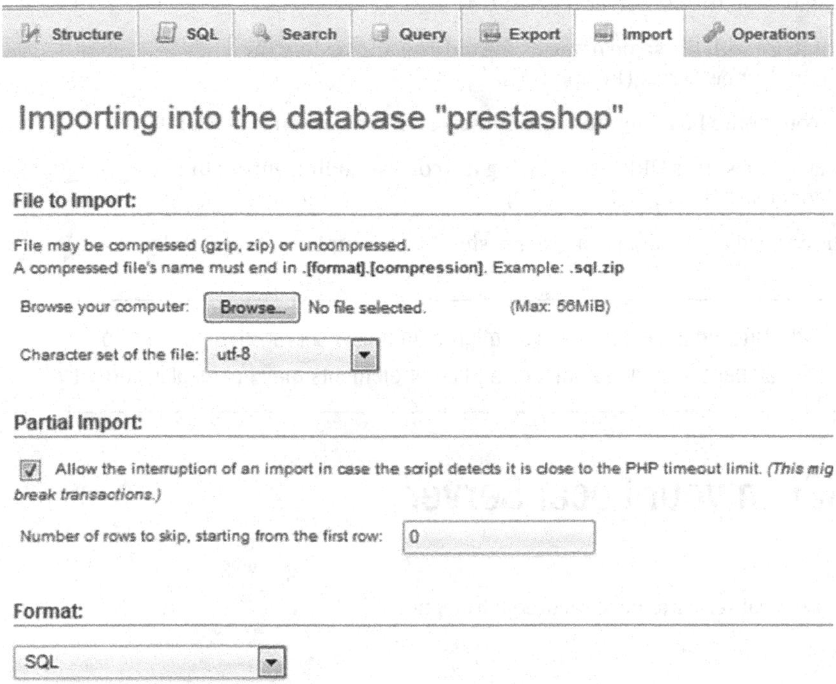

Figure 1-22. *Restoring or importing database in phpMyAdmin*

To restore a database, we visit the Import tab and browse through our `.sql` (or similar) backup files. After selecting one, we click the Go button (Figure 1-22).

It's recommended that you keep daily backups of your databases. There are different MySQL tools, such as Navicat (`www.navicat.com`),that will allow you to automatically set this up.

___

■ **Note** Backing up in DBMS is the process by which the complete structure of a database, including its data, is stored in the form of sql statements as to avoid information losses or to create restoration points.

___

1-5. Migrating from One Server to Another

Problem

You want to migrate your PS website from one hosting account or server to another.

Solution

In this case, the solution lies in the set of recipes we have seen so far.

How It Works

The migration can be accomplished following the next steps:

1. Back up your database in the old server (Recipe 1-4).

2. Create a new database with the same name as the old one and restore the previous backup in the new server (Recipe 1-4).

3. Copy and paste your entire PS folder from the old server to the new one via FTP.

4. If necessary, change the shop's URL by modifying the corresponding entries in the new server's database (Recipe 1-3).

If you follow these steps correctly, the migration process should be completed successfully.

■ **Note**   If you are using friendly URLs in the old PS and you migrate to a new server, change them to non-friendly URLs to update the database. Otherwise, images and other elements may not display correctly.

1-6. Enabling SSL in your Local Server

Problem

You want to enable SSL in your local server to have secured connections.

Solution

The Hypertext Transfer Protocol Secure (HTTPS) represents the secured version of the Hypertext Transfer Protocol (HTTP). It's commonly used by financial entities such as banks and online stores to send sensitive information (private records, passwords) over the Web. It uses a cyphering based on SSL to create a channel where an encrypted stream is sent from sender to receiver (both having a key to decrypt it), and any attack in the middle will be useless since the attacker should be incapable of decrypting that stream.

In the Web environment, the encrypted stream translates into an encrypted link, the receiver to a web server and sender to a browser.

Creating an SSL connection requires an SSL Certificate for the server. When you choose to activate SSL, you will have to complete a number of questions about the identity of your website and company. The web server then creates two cryptographic keys, a Private and a Public Key.

SSL uses a type of cryptography known as Public Key Cryptography, or Two-Key Cryptography, where two actors, sender and receiver, own Public and Private Keys. The Public one can be delivered to anyone and the latter must be kept inaccessible. Cryptographic methods guarantee that the Public-Private Key pair generated is unique so it never occurs that two different individuals share the same pair.

The main branches of Public Key Cryptography are Public Key Encryption (PKE) and Digital Signatures (DS).

In PKE, the sender uses the receiver's Public Key to encrypt the message. once encrypted, only the receiver can decrypt it using its own Private Key. Remember the receiver is the only one with access to it. Confidentiality is achieved in this manner; no one but receiver can decrypt the message.

In DS, the sender uses his or her Private Key to encrypt the message so it can be later decrypted by receiver. The identification-authenticity of the sender gets verified this way because the sender is the only one who could have encrypted the message with its Private Key.

Habitually, an SSL Certificate includes your domain name, your company name, your address, your city, your state, and your country. It also contains the expiration date of the Certificate as well as details of the Certification Authority responsible for issuing the Certificate. When a browser connects to a secure site, it will retrieve the site's SSL Certificate and check that it has not expired, it has been issued by a Certification Authority the browser trusts, and that it is being used by the website for which it has been issued. If it fails on any one of these checks, the browser will display a warning to the user letting him or her know that the site is not secured by SSL.

The Public Key is placed into a Certificate Signing Request (CSR), which is a data file also containing your details. You should then submit the CSR. During the SSL Certificate application process, the Certification Authority will validate your details and issue an SSL Certificate containing your details, allowing you to use SSL. Your web server will match your issued SSL Certificate to your Private Key. Then it will be able to establish an encrypted link between the website and your customer's web browser.

■ **Note**   In the OSI (Open System Interconnection, ISO/IEC 7490-1) model, HTTPS belongs to the application layer where several protocols for exchanging data between applications are defined. Among these protocols we can find HTTP, HTTPS, POP, SMTP, FTP, and so on.

How It Works

Enabling SSL in WAMP requires us to create an SSL certificate. For this purpose, we will install Win32OpenSSL_Light-1_1_0.exe, which can be downloaded from http://slproweb.com/download/Win32OpenSSL_Light-1_1_0.exe and can be used to create certificates.

Once we've installed the program, we go to My PC->Preferences->Advanced System Configuration->Environment Variables and add the environment variable OPENSSL_CONF, setting its value to the path of the openssl.conf file; in my case, it's C:\wamp\bin\apache\Apache2.2.21\conf\openssl.conf. This is a very sensitive file that must be configured properly with a lot of information.

Then we create the SSL certificate and its associated key. First, open the command line and type openssl; it should change to the OpenSSL console (Figure 1-23). Then execute the following steps.

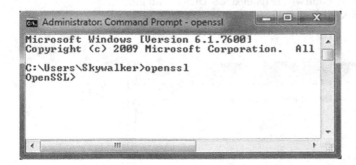

Figure 1-23. *OpenSSL console online*

■ **Note**   If the command line does not recognize the openssl command, edit the Path system environment variable adding a semicolon at the end followed by the path to the openssl executable. In my case, it is C:\OpenSSL-Win32\bin.

1. Type the following command to generate a private key:

    ```
    genrsa -des3 -out localhost.key 1024
    ```

    It will ask you for a pass phrase (Figure 1-24); do not forget it.

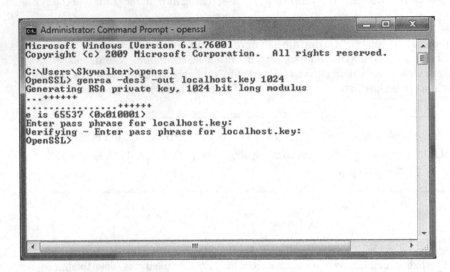

Figure 1-24. *Pass phrase request*

2. To remove the pass phrase and create a new copy, type these commands:

    ```
    copy localhost.key localhost.key.org
    rsa -in localhost.key.org -out localhost.key
    ```

    In Figure 1-25, notice that in the first line we are using a MS-DOS command; thus, we'll need to exit the openssl console to execute it. Type q to exit. Re-enter later to type the last command.

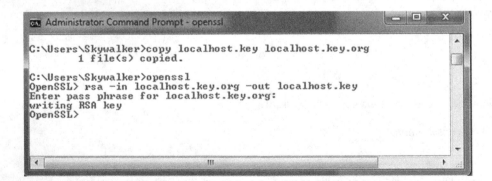

Figure 1-25. *Removing the pass phrase*

3. Create a certificate from the generated key by typing the following (see Figure 1-26):

```
req -new -x509 -nodes -sha1 -days 365 -key localhost.key -out localhost.crt
-config C:\wamp\bin\apache\Apache2.2.21\conf\openssl.cnf
```

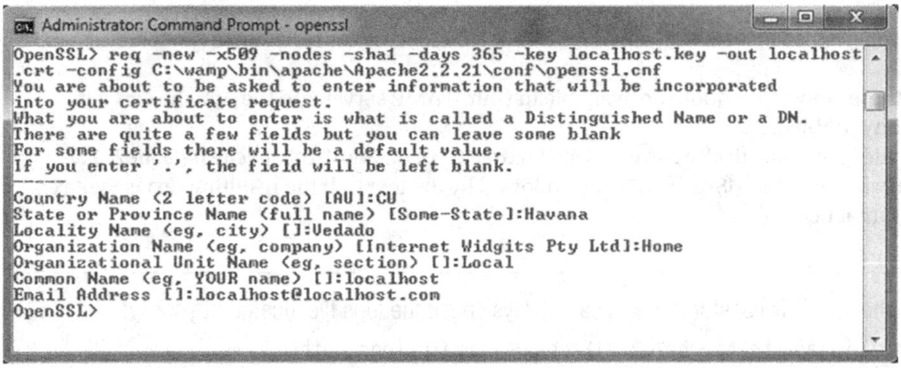

Figure 1-26. *Creating a certificate*

Note that your openssl.cnf path may be different; modify it if necessary.

4. To put some order (always important), let's create a folder named OpenSSL in the root of our WAMP server, by default it is C:/wamp/, so the final path to the new folder would be C:/wamp/OpenSSL. Inside, we'll create the subfolders certs and private.

5. In the path where you started the OpenSSL console, C:\Users\Skywalker in my case, find the files localhost.crt and localhost.key and move/copy them to the newly created certs folder. Then move the localhost.key.org file to the private folder.

6. After having created our certificate and private key and located them in a nice spot, it's time to link them to Apache. To establish this link, we need to edit the http.conf Apache file, which can be open from the WAMP daemon panel or, in my case, accessing C:\wamp\bin\apache\Apache2.2.21\conf\.

7. Uncomment the following three lines:

LoadModule ssl_module modules/mod_ssl.so

LoadModule setenvif_module modules/mod_setenvif.so

Include conf/extra/httpd-ssl.conf

8. Now open C:\wamp\bin\apache\Apache2.2.21\conf\extra\httpd-ssl.conf.

9. Change and uncomment (if necessary) the following lines:

ServerName www.example.com:443 to ServerName localhost:443

SSLCertificateFile c:/Apache2/conf/server-dsa.crt to SSLCertificateFile c:/wamp/OpenSSL/certs/localhost.crt

SSLCertificateKeyFile c:/Apache2/conf/server-dsa.key to SSLCertificateKeyFile c:/wamp/OpenSSL/certs/localhost.key

10. It's important that you update all paths written in the httpd-ssl.conf file because some may be incorrect, pointing to C:/Apache2 instead of your WAMP Apache folder. Check that out.

11. Finally, in the WAMP daemon panel, go to PHP->php.ini and uncomment the next line by removing the leading semicolon:

    ;extension=php_openssl.dll

After executing these steps, SSL should be available in your WAMP server and the Apache service should start without any problem.

To verify that all files are syntactically correct, you can drag the C:\wamp\bin\apache\Apache2.2.21\bin\httpd.exe executable into any MS-DOS window followed by the text -t. If the resulting text is Syntax OK, then all files are syntactically correct.

■ **Note** If your Apache server is not starting, you can always check the logs file located at your corresponding C:\wamp\bin\apache\Apache2.2.21\logs or C:\wamp\logs paths.

1-7. Enabling SSL in PrestaShop

Problem

You want to enable SSL in your PS website.

Solution

Assuming your sever supports SSL connections and you want to enable it in PrestaShop, you must access the Back Office and activate the Enable SSL link found under Preferences->General (Figure 1-27).

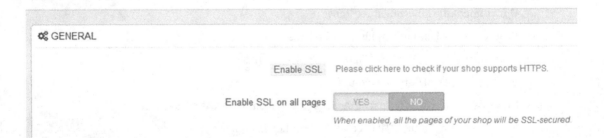

Figure 1-27. Link to activate SSL in PS

How It Works

If you are using a self-signed certificate like the one we used in the previous recipe, then we'll probably get a warning message (Figure 1-28) that would depend on the browser being used.

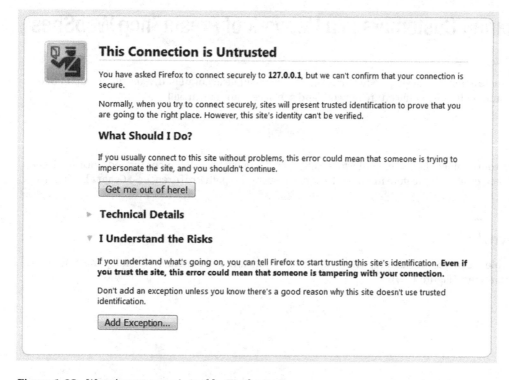

Figure 1-28. *Warning message issued by Firefox*

Since we are in a testing environment, we add the exception and move forward. To avoid such warning, you would need a certificate from a trusted third-party organization. When activating SSL, you will see the HTTPS protocol displayed in the browser's bar (Figure 1-29).

Figure 1-29. *SSL activated*

Using a self-signed certificate, you are telling the browser "I'm OK, trust me," but he's obviously not buying that. Using a third-party certificate (issued by a trusted organization) would be like having them telling the browser "Trust him, he is OK." Depending on how well-known this organization is, he may trust you. Organizations like GeoTrust or Symantec are all devoted to providing these digital certificates.

1-8. Sharing Customers in a Network of PrestaShop WebSites

Problem

You want to create a network of shops where customers have a single account and, after signing up in one site, they become customers of the entire network and can access any site at will.

Solution

The solution to our problem lies in the multistore feature, which PrestaShop has incorporated since version 1.5. You can enable or disable this feature in the Back Office following the path `Preferences->General->Enable MultiStore`.

How It Works

Once you enable the multistore feature, a new tab named Multistore will appear on the left panel under Advanced Parameters (Figure 1-30).

Figure 1-30. *Multistore area*

In this tab, we'll create a new shop group named HDE and activate the Share Customers feature for it. To create a new group, click the Add a new Shop Group button on the upper right corner and then fill out the Shop group name field as shown in Figure 1-31. The new group will now appear on the Shop group list.

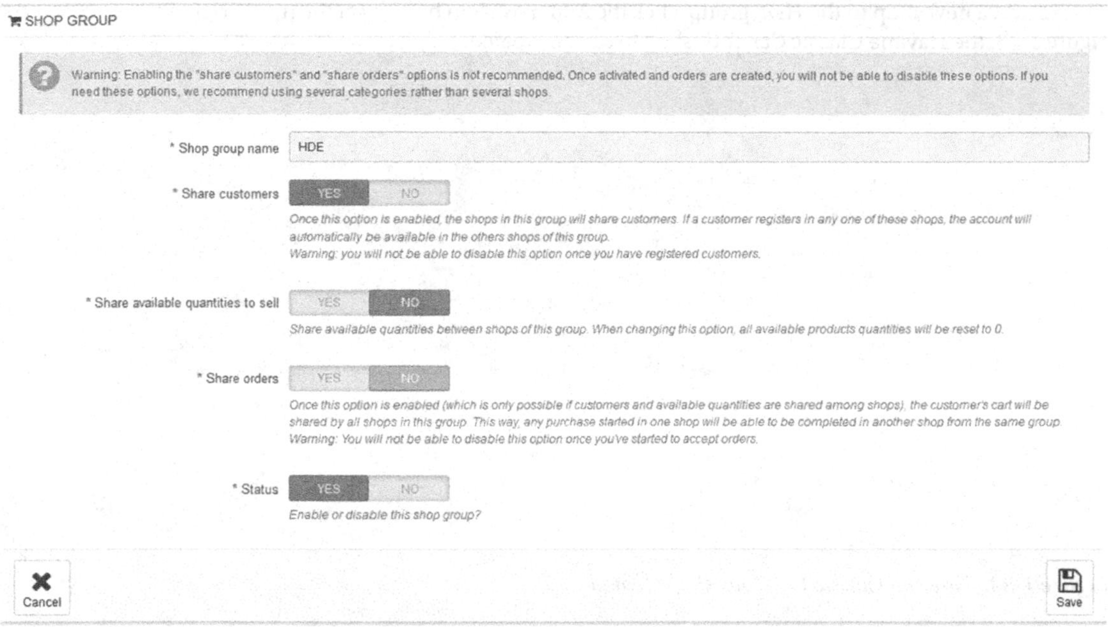

🛒 SHOP GROUP

❓ Warning: Enabling the "share customers" and "share orders" options is not recommended. Once activated and orders are created, you will not be able to disable these options. If you need these options, we recommend using several categories rather than several shops.

* Shop group name   HDE

* Share customers   [YES] [NO]

Once this option is enabled, the shops in this group will share customers. If a customer registers in any one of these shops, the account will automatically be available in the others shops of this group.
Warning: you will not be able to disable this option once you have registered customers.

* Share available quantities to sell   [YES] [NO]

Share available quantities between shops of this group. When changing this option, all available products quantities will be reset to 0.

* Share orders   [YES] [NO]

Once this option is enabled (which is only possible if customers and available quantities are shared among shops), the customer's cart will be shared by all shops in this group. This way, any purchase started in one shop will be able to be completed in another shop from the same group.
Warning: You will not be able to disable this option once you've started to accept orders.

* Status   [YES] [NO]

Enable or disable this shop group?

✖ Cancel   💾 Save

Figure 1-31. *HDE shop group being created*

Now that we have created the shop group representing our network, we can complete it with new shops (Figure 1-32).

MULTISTORE (2)

ID ▼▲	Shop group ▼▲
1	Default
2	HDE

Figure 1-32. *Shop group added*

■ **Note**   PS allows to share not only customers between different stores but also quantities and orders. The notion of shop group permits the partition of your shop into different shops, each with unique attributes.

To add a new shop to the HDE group, click the Add new shop button on the upper right corner. In Figure 1-33, the Havana Classic Car Tour shop has been created.

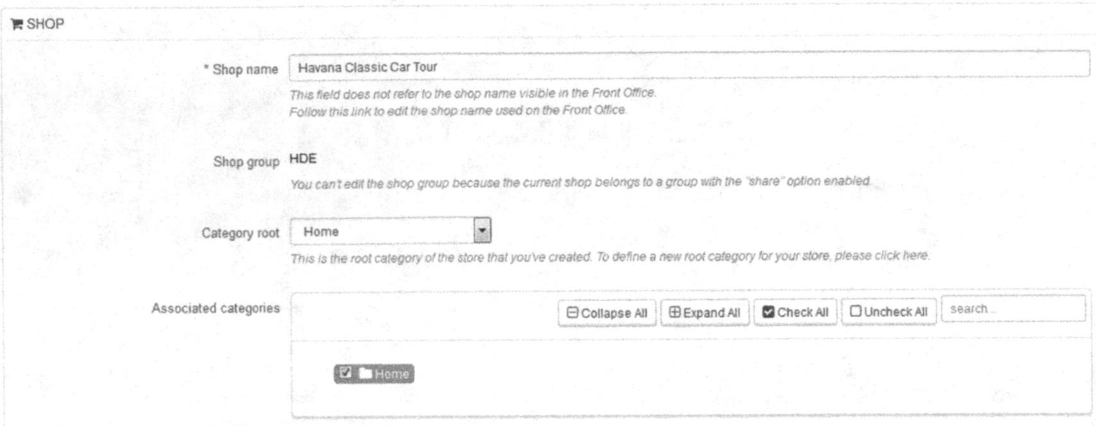

SHOP

* Shop name — Havana Classic Car Tour

This field does not refer to the shop name visible in the Front Office.
Follow this link to edit the shop name used on the Front Office.

Shop group — HDE

You can't edit the shop group because the current shop belongs to a group with the "share" option enabled.

Category root — Home

This is the root category of the store that you've created. To define a new root category for your store, please click here.

Associated categories — Collapse All Expand All Check All Uncheck All search...

Home

Figure 1-33. *Havana Classic Car Tour shop created*

Fill out the necessary information and set the Import Data field to Yes state. Importing data from one store to the other will give us access to several PS tables. We'll also set different themes for each shop seeking a distinction between them.

Now we see the newly created shop on the multistore tree (Figure 1-34). Click it to go to the shops table.

In the shops table, we find the Havana Classic Car Tour row. Click the Main URL for this shop column to define a URL as shown in Figure 1-35.

MULTISTORE TREE

- Default
  - MyShop
    - localhost/prestashop/
- HDE
  - Havana Classic Car Tour

Figure 1-34. *Newly created shop in multistore tree*

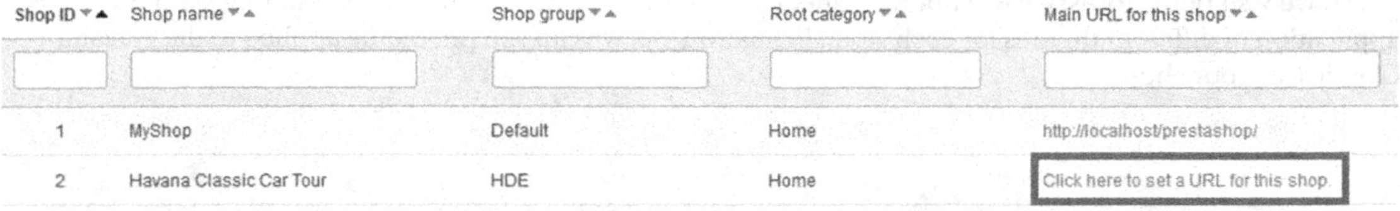

Shop ID ▼▲	Shop name ▼▲	Shop group ▼▲	Root category ▼▲	Main URL for this shop ▼▲
1	MyShop	Default	Home	http://localhost/prestashop/
2	Havana Classic Car Tour	HDE	Home	Click here to set a URL for this shop.

Figure 1-35. *Shops table*

Remember, in this example, we are working from a local server; therefore, our domain will be localhost. The Virtual URL field provides the opportunity of setting a virtual URL, that is, a URL that doesn't really exist in the server—in this case, havanaclassiccartour; this can be seen in Figure 1-36.

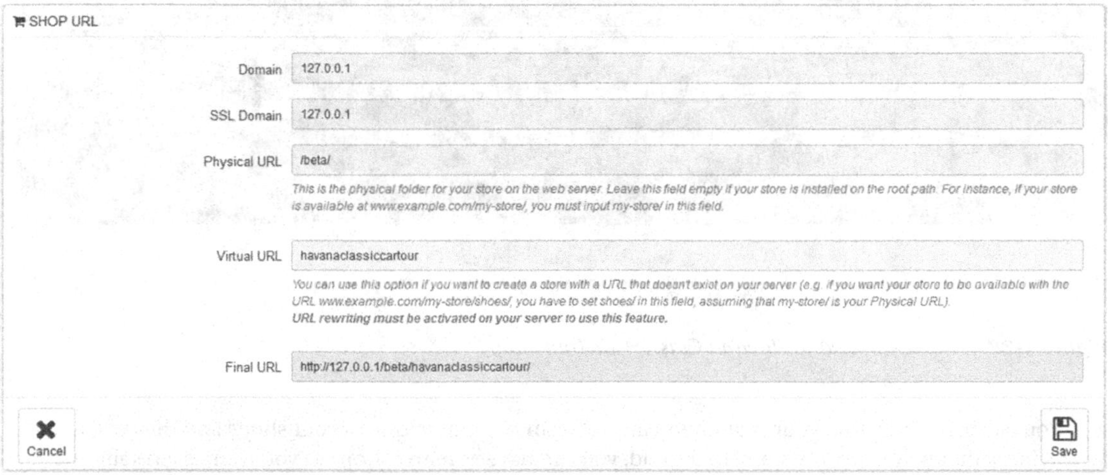

Figure 1-36. *Defining URL for the newly created shop*

To finish, we just need to edit the other shop, fill out the Virtual URL field with the prestashop text, select a different theme, and move it from the Default group to HDE (Figure 1-37).

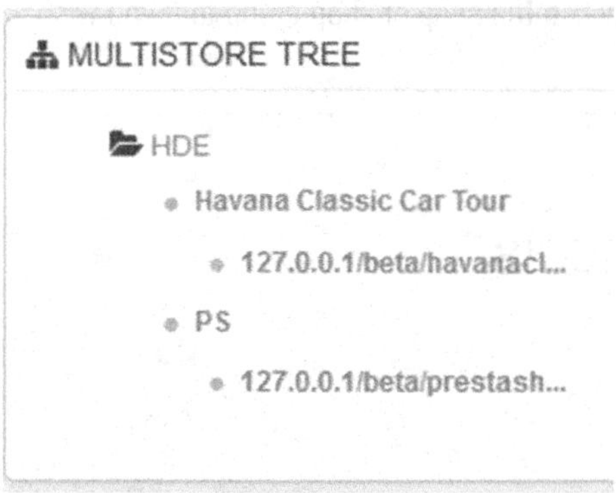

Figure 1-37. *HDE group fully created*

If we visit both stores, we will notice immediately a bunch of visual differences resulting from the application of different themes for each store. In Figure 1-38, we can see the theme applied to the Havana Classic Car Tour shop.

Figure 1-38. *Theme applied to Havana Classic Car Tour shop*

You can also verify that your customers can create an account in one of your shops and they will have access indistinctively from any store. In the end, you can have as many shops as you want, each selling a different set of products (remember categories are selected prior to shop creation in multistore) and conforming a network of websites with common credentials for customers.

■ **Note**   The multistore feature allows you to manage multiple stores at the same time. For each one, you can define which modules are enabled/disabled and you can select theme, products, and so on. The Back Office incorporates a drop-down box on the upper left corner when you choose the shop or shop group that you wish to configure at present time.

1-9. Selling Services instead of Products

Problem

You want to sell services instead of tangible products.

Solution

A service does not require a warehouse, quantities defined, or a shipping process. It's something that you sell and is intangible; therefore, PS treats it as a virtual product. In the product creation page, you can set a product as virtual (Figure 1-39).

Figure 1-39. *Product creation page*

Virtual products are usually services, bookings, or anything that does not involve a physical presence.

How It Works

When you set a product as virtual, the shipping tab on the left panel disappears. This is what you would expect from a product that is a service, booking, or anything similar.

The problem is that the combinations tab also disappears and combinations provide the possibility of changing a product's price dependent on the subset of attributes selected. For instance, you may have a tour on an American Classic Car through Havana product for $60 and attributes place, time, guided service, and so on. You want to increase the price to $75 if the customer selects the guided service attribute. In that scenario, you would need the combinations tab.

A better alternative for working with services, booking products, and other similar items is to create them as standard products, disable their shipping, build your own PS theme (erasing all trace of shipping), and modify the necessary e-mail templates. In this book, we'll see how to accomplish this task recipe by recipe.

■ **Note**   Selecting the Virtual Product option also activates a Virtual Product tab on the left panel where you can upload a file associated with that product.

1-10. Disabling Shipping

Problem

You want to disable shipping for your standard products.

Solution

If you have a standard product that can't be shipped, maybe a booking service or something similar, you can disable shipping by creating a Free Shipping carrier and defining it as the only carrier for that product.

How It Works

To create a carrier, you need to access the PS Back Office, go to `Shipping->Carriers` (Figure 1-40) on the right upper corner, and click Add new carrier. In case none of your products includes shipping, you could leave a single carrier named Free.

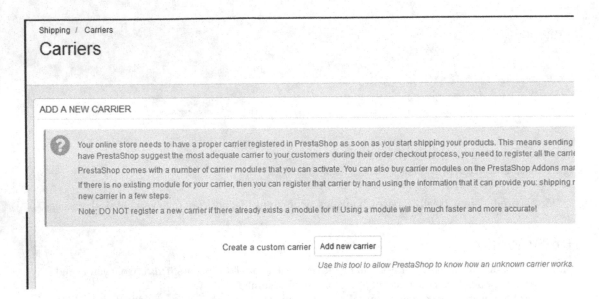

Figure 1-40. *Add new carrier*

Our goal is to add a custom carrier, so we click the Add new carrier button, and it will take us to a multiform where we'll input every detail regarding our new carrier (Figure 1-41).

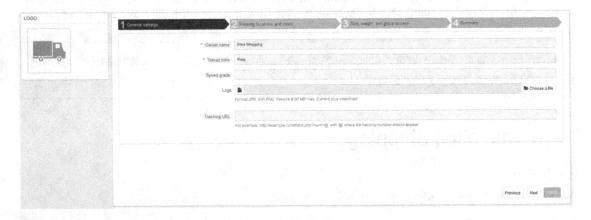

Figure 1-41. *Multiform to configure your new custom carrier*

We name our new carrier Free Shipping and set its Transit time value to Free, leaving the remaining fields empty, as shown in Figure 1-42. In the second form, we activate the Free Shipping option.

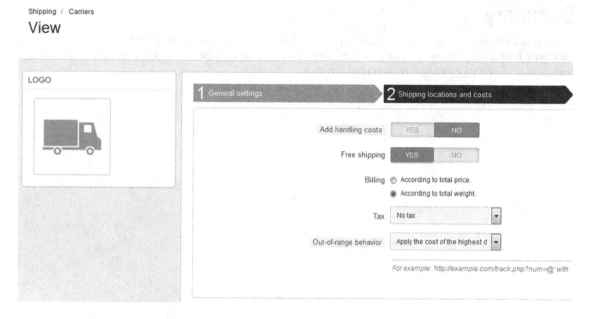

Figure 1-42. *Free shipping activated for new carrier*

In Step 2, we click the Finish button and our free custom carrier is created. We don't need to move forward since the last two steps demand the configuration of fields associated with shipping costs.

We can set our free carrier as the default carrier if we go to Shipping->Preferences and select it from the Default Carrier drop-down list (Figure 1-43).

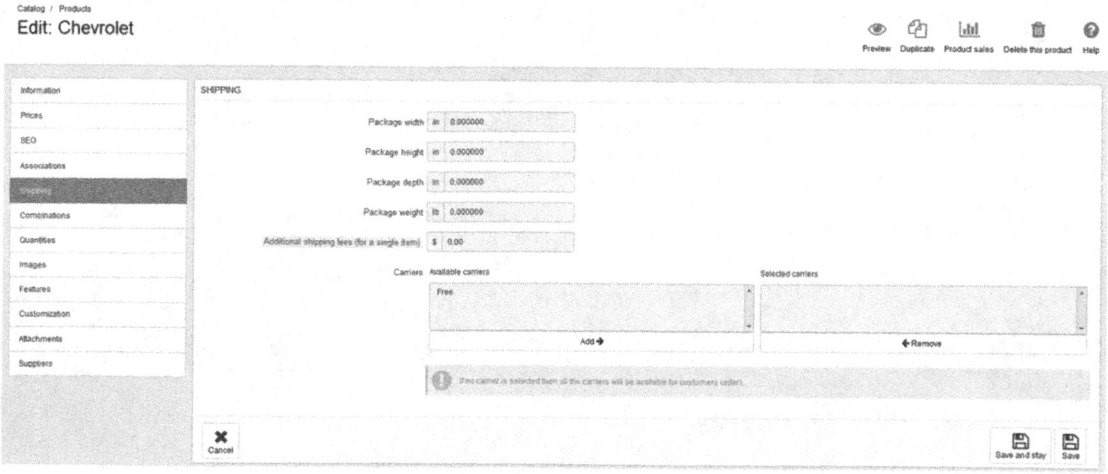

Figure 1-43. *Defining carrier for a product*

In case you want a subset of your products to have free shipping, you can always edit those products, go to the Shipping panel, and define the carrier you want for them.

Summary

Throughout this chapter, we examined several recipes that show us how to appropriately install and configure PrestaShop. In the following chapter, we will start diving into the world of module development, a feature that allows PS extensibility and customization.

CHAPTER 2

∎ ∎ ∎

Module Development

Modules represent the manner in which PrestaShop allows us to alter or add functionality to our websites. We can find modules to complete online payments (Stripe, PayPal, and so on), enhance or change front-end features like the slider and top menu, or completely transform the original PS idea and turn it into a booking site, a travel agency, and so forth. On the PrestaShop home page, most components you see (slider, search box, top menu, popular products list, and so on) are modules that can be customized, enabled or disabled.

When you are in need of adding certain functionalities to your PS website, you usually encounter two alternatives. You can locate and buy the module that provides the required functionality or you can develop it yourself. In this chapter, we'll describe various recipes that will allow you to do the following:

- Create a Hello World PS module displayed at the header

- Position your module

- Transplant your module

- Create your own hook

- Add a configuration link to your module

- Create a YouTube module

- Configure your PS site using SQL queries during module installation

- Create a module for sending e-mail notifications after order confirmation

- Add more information to order e-mail notifications

- Change CSS styles through a module

∎ **Note**   If you want to change the way a module looks on your PS site, you can edit the `.tpl` Smarty files associated with your current theme folder following the path `theme_folder/modules/your_module`.

© Arnaldo Pérez Castaño 2017
A. P. Castaño, *PrestaShop Recipes*, DOI 10.1007/978-1-4842-2574-5_2

2-1. Create a Hello World PS Module Displayed at the Header

Problem

You want to create a module that displays the Hello World on the header when installed.

Solution

All modules are located in a folder named modules at the root of your PrestaShop package. They are composed of various files all contained within their folder in the path modules/your_module_name, where all their files should be. Every module must include these three files:

1. config.xml: the cache configuration file

2. logo.png (for PS 1.5+), logo.jpg, or logo.gif (up to PS 1.4): icon file that represents the module in the Back Office. If the module is operational for both 1.4 and 1.5+, then logo.png and logo.gif must be included. Dimensions should be 16x16 pixels.

3. your_module_name.php: the main PHP file. It must have the same name as the module's folder and it handles most processing.

The config file is automatically generated by PS when installing the module, so you don't really need to worry about it. This leaves us with two files that must be created or included on module development.

How It Works

To start, let's create a helloworld folder inside the modules directory at the root of your PS package. Next, we create the main PHP file (helloworld.php) and the module's logo (logo.gif), as shown in Figure 2-1.

Figure 2-1. *Files of the helloworld module*

All modules start with a simple constant test, which verifies the existence of PrestaShop as CMS handling files (Listing 2-1); this prevents malicious visitors from loading them directly and eventually getting access to the code.

Listing 2-1. Checking for PS Constant

```php
<?php
if(!defined('PS_VERSION_'))
        exit;
```

The module itself is a PHP class that extends from the PS Module class (Listing 2-2); the name must be written in CamelCase and it must be the same as the folder's name. In general, your module can inherit from the Module class or from any of its specialized descendants (PaymentModule, ModuleGraph, and so on).

Listing 2-2. Declaring the Module's Class

```php
<?php
if(!defined('_PS_VERSION_'))
        exit;

class HelloWorld extends Module {
}
```

■ **Note**   The name of the module's folder is the same as the module and cannot include any spaces—only alphanumerical characters, the hyphen, and underscore (all lowercase).

Now it's time to start filling the HelloWorld class. We start by creating the constructor (Listing 2-3).

Listing 2-3. Class Constructor

```php
class HelloWorld extends Module {

public function __construct()
{
            $this->name = 'helloworld';
            $this->tab = 'front_office_features';
            $this->version = '1.0.0';
            $this->author = 'Arnaldo Perez Castano';
            $this->need_instance = 0;
            $this->ps_versions_compliancy = array('min' => '1.6', 'max' => _PS_VERSION_);
            $this->bootstrap = true;

            parent::__construct();

            $this->displayName = $this->l('Hello World');
            $this->description = $this->l('Display Hello World text');

            $this->confirmUninstall = $this->l('Are you sure you want to uninstall?');

            if (!Configuration::get('HELLOWORLD_NAME'))
              $this->warning = $this->l('No name provided');
}
}
```

In the constructor, we define values for several attributes of the Module class.

- Name: must be the same as the module's folder name, in lowercase and following the same rules

- Tab: the section in the Back Office->Modules that will contain this module. Since we are creating a front-end module, our tab is front_office_features.

- Version: the module's version, as a string

- Author: the module's author, as a string

- Need_instance: indicates whether the module's class needs to be loaded when displaying the Modules page in the Back Office. A value of 0 turns it off; a value of 1 turns it on. It's usually turned on for modules that must display a warning message in the Modules page; leaving it like that unjustified could lead to higher time consumptions when loading the Modules page.

- Ps_versions_compliancy: indicates what versions of PrestaShop are compatible with the module

- BootStrap: indicates whether template files correspond to PrestaShop 1.6's bootstrap or not

The module should be visible now in the Modules page on PS Back Office as illustrated in Figure 2-2. We continue the development process by making a call to the parent's constructor (Module class). This call must be done after creating the $this->name variable and before calling the translation method $this->l().

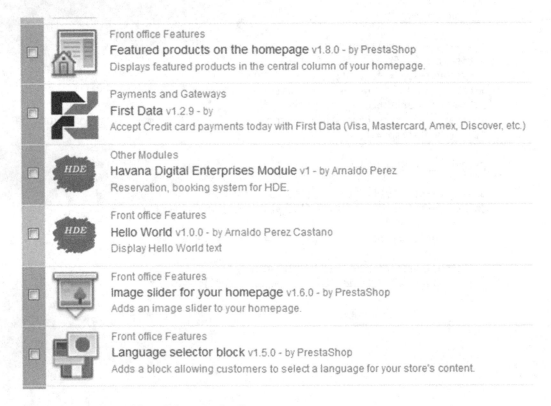

Figure 2-2. Helloworld module on Back Office

After calling the parent's constructor, we set a group of strings that will be use for messages or simply displaying text in PrestaShop.

- displayName: the name displayed in the module's list in the Back Office

- description: a description of the module, shown in the module's list in the Back Office

- confirmUninstall: a message that appears before uninstalling the module

To be able to install our module from the module's list, we need to define the install() and uninstall() methods at the same level as the class constructor. Through these Boolean methods, we can determine what happens when the administrator installs or uninstalls some module. We'll keep it simple for now, just incorporating a call to the parent's install, uninstall method and registering it to the top hook in the first case (Listing 2-4). If something fails, the module will not be installed.

Listing 2-4. Install and Uninstall Methods

```
public function install() {
        if (!parent::install() ||
                !$this->registerHook('top'))
                return false;
        return true;
}

public function uninstall() {
        if (!parent::uninstall())
                return false;
        return true;
}
```

We'll see more on PS hooks throughout this chapter. For the moment, we just need to know that having your module hooked up is equivalent to having a channel to insert some code in your site at a certain moment or location; it could be when displaying the header (top), when loading the left column, at the center of your homepage, and so on.

Taking into account that we have already attached our module to the top hook, we just need to define the code to be executed when the module is enabled (Listing 2-5).

Listing 2-5. Top Hook Method

```
public function hookTop($params){
global $smarty;
return $this->display(__FILE__, 'helloworld.tpl');
}
```

The name of a hooking method starts with the hook prefix followed by the name of the hook itself, top in this case. PrestaShop uses the Smarty web template system for adding logic, loops, and variables in .tpl files that are eventually rendered as HTML pages. In order to interact with Smarty, we define the global variable $smarty. The display method then returns the content of the template file helloworld.tpl representing the visuality of the module (Listing 2-6).

Listing 2-6. Helloworld.tpl Smarty File

```
<div class="col-sm-3">
        <h2> Hello World </h2><br>
        <h4> havanaclassicartour.com </h4>
</div>
```

Now we can proceed with the module's installation by clicking the Install button as seen in Figure 2-3.

Figure 2-3. *Button to install module*

Once we click the Install button, we'll be prompted with a warning message asking us to confirm that the module can be trusted. According to PrestaShop, the only trusted modules are those from their official market place (`addons.prestashop.com`) or from one of their partner's market place. Since we are developing this module and we know it's reliable, we'll click the Proceed with the Installation button and get the module installed (Figure 2-4).

Figure 2-4. *Module installed*

After the installation has been completed, we can see the module displayed on the header as illustrated in Figure 2-5.

Figure 2-5. *Module displayed on header*

In this recipe, we learned how to create a simple module that displays the "Hello World" text on the header. Modules allow us to add functionality and configure PS without the need to modify any core files, thus making our stores more flexible and easier to extend.

2-2. Positioning Your Module

Problem

You want to change the position or order in which your modules are being displayed.

Solution

To alter the order in which your modules are being displayed, you need to visit PS Back Office and then go to (Modules and Services)->Positions. To exemplify, let's try to move the Hello World module we just created on the last recipe from one position to another.

How It Works

On the Positions page, we input "top" in the "Search for a hook" text field to the right. Remember that's the hook where we attached our module. Once you have located it, drag it up and put it under the Cart Block module (Figure 2-6).

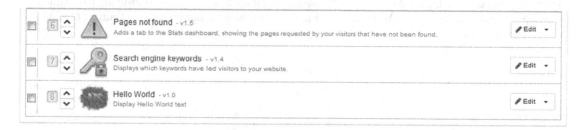

Figure 2-6. *Locating the Hello World module on Positions page*

Now you can reload your PS home page and see how the "Hello World" text is shown elsewhere as depicted in Figure 2-7.

Figure 2-7. *Module after changing its position*

Modules are arranged in a linear form so you can imagine them line up and have the predecessor and successor of your module defining its position over that line. In the previous case, we set the Hello World module after the Cart Block module and before the Top Horizontal Menu. That's exactly where it lies on the header—after the Reservations button (Cart) and before the Top Menu.

Visually the Cart Block appears to be after the Hello World module, but that's not really the case. The imaginary line of modules in the top hook starts with the logo and continues with the Contact/User Info module, the Cart Block module, the Hello World module, and finally the Top Menu Module.

2-3. Transplanting Your Module

Problem

You want to transplant a module to attach it to another hook.

Solution

Transplanting a module is the process by which you move it from one hook to another. Accomplishing this task requires you to unhook your module and attach it to the new hook.

How It Works

First, we need to unhook the module we want to transplant (Figure 2-8). We can do this in the Back Office following (`Modules and services`)->`Positions` and then searching for our module and editing the entry that corresponds to it.

Figure 2-8. *Unhooking a module*

Once you have unhooked the module, you click the Transplant module button on the upper right corner of the Positions page, as shown in Figure 2-9.

Figure 2-9. *Transplant a module button*

On the Transplant page, we find the module that we want to transplant (Figure 2-10), Hello World in our case, and indicate the hook to which we need it attached.

Figure 2-10. *Transplanting the Hello World module in the top hook*

On this page, you also have the option of specifying a comma separated list of files for which you don't want the module selected to be displayed, as seen in Figure 2-11.

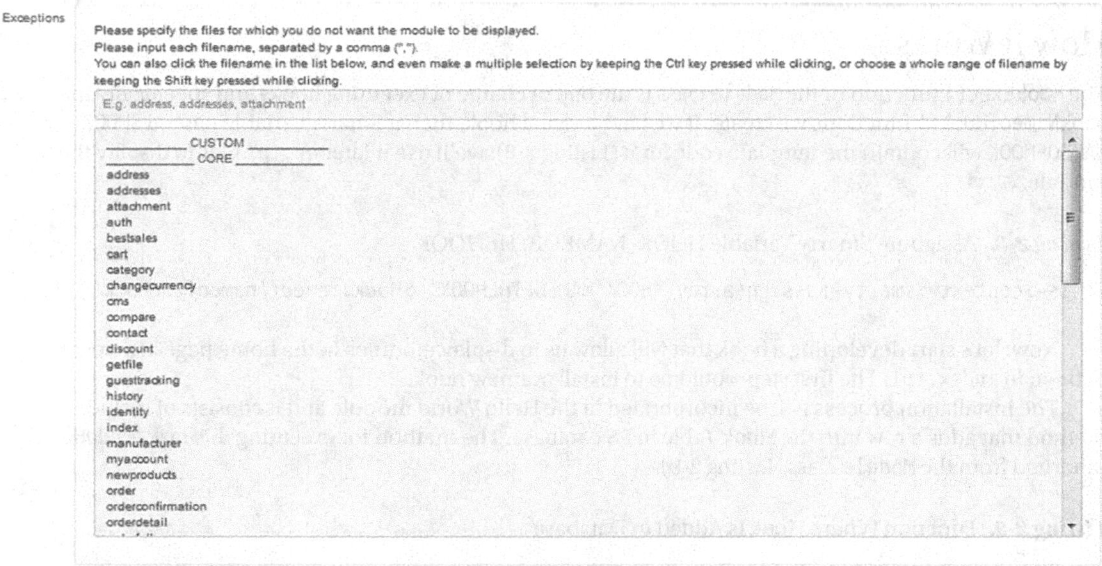

Figure 2-11. *Specifying files for which the module will not be displayed*

After clicking the Save button, we'll see that our Hello World is back to the hook it was attached and the transplantation process has been completed.

2-4. Creating Your Own Hook

Problem

You want to create your own hook so modules can attach to it.

Solution

Hooks can be divided into two main categories—the visual hooks and the action hooks.

When "hooked up" to a visual hook, you can display content in the location where that hook was declared in your templates. The top hook, for instance, that we used in the Hello World module is tied to a variable $HOOK_TOP declared on the page header so its visual content is displayed there (Listing 2-7).

Listing 2-7. Fragment of the header.tpl Template File Where the Top Hook Is Declared

```
{if isset($HOOK_TOP)}
{$HOOK_TOP}
{/if}
```

Action hooks on the other side merely run module's code at certain moments during PS execution. These types of hooks are usually included in controllers and classes to manipulate any data they might return. The cart hook, for example, is executed in the Cart.php class right after a cart is updated or created, and the createAccount hook in authentication.php is called right after the client account is created.

How It Works

The hookExec() function in the Module class is the one in charge of executing hooks and specifically the hookNameofHook() functions we create. If we have a visual hook, then a Smarty variable named $HOOK_NAMEOFHOOK will contain the template code for it (Listing 2-8); we'll use it later in .tpl files to display the module.

Listing 2-8. Assigning Smarty Variable HOOK_NAMEOFTHEHOOK

```
$this->context->smarty->assign(array('HOOK_NAMEOFTHEHOOK'=>Hook::exec('nameofthehook')));
```

Now, let's start developing a hook that will allow us to display modules in the home page at a position defined in index.tpl. The first step would be to install our new hook.

The installation process will be incorporated in the Hello World module and it consists of including a method that adds a row into the Hook Table in PS database. The method for executing this task is addHook(), inherited from the Module class (Listing 2-9).

Listing 2-9. Function Where Hook Is Added in Database

```
protected function addHook() {
        // Checking the module does not exist
        $exists = Db::getInstance()->getRow('
                        SELECT name
                        FROM '._DB_PREFIX_.'hook
                        WHERE name = "homepage"
                        ');
        // If it does not exist
        if (!$exists) {
                $query = "INSERT INTO "._DB_PREFIX_."hook (`name`, `title`, `description`)
                VALUES ('homepage', 'HomePage', 'Hooks in the homepage');";
                if(Db::getInstance()->Execute($query))
                        return true;
                else
                        return false;
        }
        else return true;
}
```

The method checks that no module with the same name exists; if that's the case, then an insert statement in an SQL query adds the module to the database.

■ **Note** If you have the Hello World module already installed from the previous recipe, you need to uninstall it and then install it again so the addHook() function is executed and the hook created on database.

Now we need to define the method that will be executed when our new hook is called (Listing 2-10).

Listing 2-10. Method Attached to Our New Hook

```
public function hookHomePage($params)
{
        global $smarty;
        return $this->display(__FILE__ , 'helloworld.tpl');
}
```

Then we need to override the IndexController located at controllers/front/. We modify the initContent() method assigning the Smarty variable $HOOK_HOMEPAGE (Listing 2-11).

■ **Note** Overriding is the process by which PS substitutes a core file by another placed in the override folder on your package root. The path to such file must recreate the same structure that the original file possesses. For instance, the IndexController.php file would be override in the folder override\controllers\front.

Listing 2-11. initContent() Method with Smarty Variable Assigned

```
public function initContent()
{
parent::initContent();
$this->addJS(_THEME_JS_DIR_.'index.js');

$this->context->smarty->assign(array('HOOK_HOME'=> Hook::exec('displayHome'),
'HOOK_HOME_TAB' => Hook::exec('displayHomeTab'),
'HOOK_HOME_TAB_CONTENT' => Hook::exec('displayHomeTabContent'),
'HOOK_HOMEPAGE' => Hook::exec('homepage'),
));

$this->setTemplate(_PS_THEME_DIR_.'index.tpl');
}
```

Finally, we just need to define the place where we'll put our Smarty variable in the index.tpl template file. In our case, we set it near the footer as shown in Listing 2-12. The result on the front end is shown in Figure 2-12.

Listing 2-12. Index.tpl template File

```
<div class="row" style="padding:15px">
<iframe width="100%" height="500"
src="http://www.youtube.com/embed/LlXAznDIRvo">
</iframe>
{$HOOK_HOMEPAGE}
</div></div>
{if isset($HOOK_HOME) && $HOOK_HOME|trim}
        <div class="clearfix pre-footer">
                <div class="container">
                {$HOOK_HOME}
                </div>
        </div>
{/if}
```

Figure 2-12. *Module tied to our new hook in the home page*

In this recipe, we showed how to create a new hook from scratch. Notice that the hook could have been added to the database without any need for an intermediary module, using phpMyAdmin and the INSERT SQL statement applied in the addHook() function.

■ **Note**   If you have any problem displaying the module, go to Preferences->Performance and clear the cache; also try reinstalling the module.

2-5. Adding a Configuration Link to Your Module

Problem

You want to add a Configure link to your module allowing users to customize it.

Solution

At some point, you have probably seen the Configure link located in the right side of each row on the module list. If you would like to add that link to your module, then you need to implement the getContent() method in your main class. In this recipe, we'll modify the Hello World module code so the text it shows can be customized in the Back Office when the user presses the Configure link.

How It Works

First, we'll add a text variable in the constructor of the HelloWorld class; we'll use it as the name of the field that will hold the text of the module in the database (Listing 2-13).

Listing 2-13. Constructor with New Text Variable

```
public function __construct()
{
            $this->name = 'helloworld';
            $this->tab = 'front_office_features';
            $this->version = '1.0.0';
            $this->text = 'mod_text';
            $this->author = 'Arnaldo Perez Castano';
            $this->need_instance = 0;
            $this->ps_versions_compliancy = array('min' => '1.6', 'max' => _PS_VERSION_);
            $this->bootstrap = true;

            parent::__construct();

            $this->displayName = $this->l('Hello World');
            $this->description = $this->l('Display Hello World text');

            $this->confirmUninstall = $this->l('Are you sure you want to uninstall?');
    }
```

Next, we define the getContent() method (Listing 2-14).

Listing 2-14. The getContent() Method

```
public function getContent()
{
if (Tools::isSubmit('submit'))
{
Configuration::updateValue($this->text, Tools::getValue('our_message'));
}
$this->displayForm();
return $this->_html;
}
```

After having defined the getContent() method, we are able to see the Configure link on the right side of our module's row in the module's list (Figure 2-13).

The getContent() method is the first to be called when we click the Configure link. Consequently, it's the correct place to update any value that might have been submitted through a form in the configuration page.

This is the purpose of the if statement inside the method. Check whether a submit is in place and, if that's the case, update the value on the database with the value of a field named our_message on a form we'll present shortly.

Front office Features
Hello World v1.0.0 - by Arnaldo Perez Castano
Display Hello World text

Configure

Figure 2-13. *Module with Configure link*

The displayForm() method is shown in Listing 2-15.

Listing 2-15. The displayForm() Method

```
private function displayForm()
{
        $this->_html .= '
        <form action="'.$_SERVER['REQUEST_URI'].'" method="post">
                <label>'.$this->l('Hello World Message').'</label>
                <div class="margin-form">
                        <input type="text" name="our_message" />
                </div><br>
                <input type="submit" name="submit" value="'.$this->l('Update').'"
                class="button" />
        </form>';
}
```

If we now click the Configure link, we'll be taken to the configuration page of our Hello World module, as illustrated in Figure 2-14.

■ **Note**   The Configuration object is a PrestaShop native object incorporated as a middle layer between the developer and database. It interacts with the ps_configuration table and eases the module settings management by storing settings in PS databases using different methods and eliminating the need to write SQL queries.

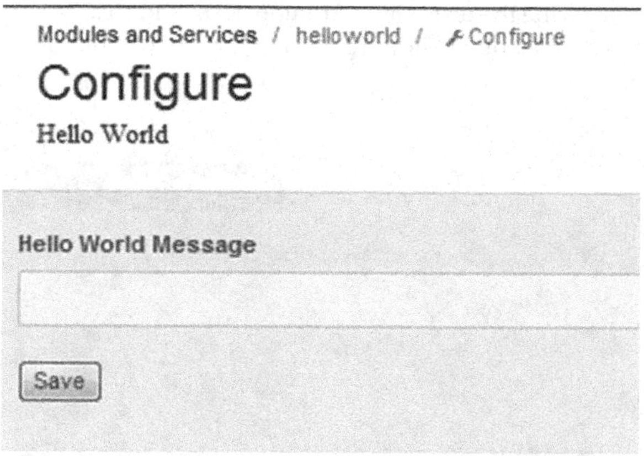

Modules and Services / helloworld / ⚙ Configure

Configure

Hello World

Hello World Message

[   ]

[Save]

Figure 2-14. *Configuration page for Hello World module*

To get the value saved in the module's configuration page, we need to link it to the file template through the hookTop method using a Smarty variable. The modification is shown in Listing 2-16.

Listing 2-16. Modification to the hookTop Method

```
public function hookTop($params)
    {
            global $smarty;

            $smarty->assign(
                            array(
                                'msg' => Configuration::get($this->text.'_message'),
                        )
                );
            return $this->display(__FILE__, 'helloworld.tpl');
    }
```

We'll also need to modify the helloworld.tpl file to display the $msg Smarty variable containing the value obtained from the database (Listing 2-17).

Listing 2-17. Modification to helloworld.tpl File

```
<div class="col-sm-3">
        <h2> {$msg} </h2><br>
        <h4> havanaclassicartour.com </h4>
</div>
```

To conclude, we test our new configuration page by saving the text "Hello Arnaldo, HDE and HCCT (Havana Classic Car Tour)" and verifying that it's later displayed on the home page as shown in Figure 2-15.

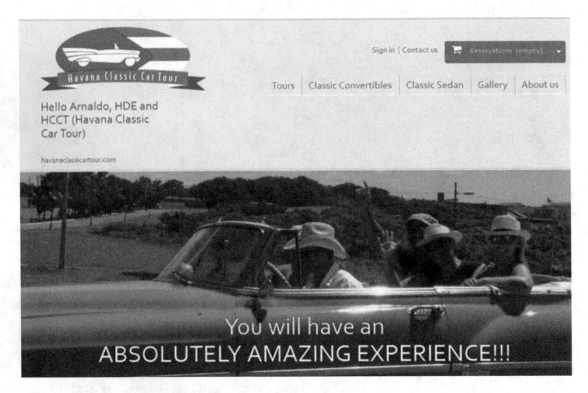

Figure 2-15. *Configuration page for Hello World module*

■ **Note**   The Configuration::get('variable') method retrieves a value from the database identified by "variable". The Configuration::updateValue('variable', $v) updates an existing database variable with the $v value. If the variable doesn't exist, it's created with $v as its value.

2-6. Creating a YouTube Module

Problem

You want to create a module that allows you to show YouTube videos on your home page and define which video is displayed.

Solution

If you are starting your own business, then most likely you have created a YouTube channel with multiple videos related to your services or products. It's a usual practice to create such a channel and add videos that will help get people interested in your business. To create the YouTube module, we'll make use of the set of skills acquired in prior recipes (create module, configure link, own hook).

How It Works

In order to simplify the development process, we'll copy and paste the helloworld folder of the module we just created and rename it "youtube", transforming it into the module we need by changing any HelloWorld references to YouTube. Its file structure should resemble Figure 2-16.

Name	Date	Type	Size	Tags
logo.gif	1/2/2002 9:45 AM	GIF image	43 KB	
logo.png	1/2/2002 9:45 AM	PNG image	79 KB	
youtube.php	1/2/2002 9:45 AM	JetBrains PhpStorm	3 KB	
youtube.tpl	1/2/2002 7:21 AM	TPL File	1 KB	

Figure 2-16. *File structure of YouTube module*

The code of the main PHP class is shown in Listing 2-18.

Listing 2-18. YouTube Module Main Class

```
class YouTube extends Module {

        public function __construct()
        {
                $this->name = 'youtube';
                $this->tab = 'front_office_features';
                $this->version = '1.0.0';
                $this->author = 'Arnaldo Perez Castano';
                $this->need_instance = 0;
                $this->ps_versions_compliancy = array('min' => '1.6', 'max' => _PS_VERSION_);
                $this->bootstrap = true;

                parent::__construct();

                $this->displayName = $this->l('YouTube');
                $this->description = $this->l('Display YouTube videos');

                $this->confirmUninstall = $this->l('Are you sure you want to uninstall?');
        }

        public function install()
        {
                if (!parent::install() ||
                        !$this->registerHook('homepage'))
                        return false;
                return true;
        }
```

```php
    public function uninstall()
    {
            if (!parent::uninstall())
                    return false;
            return true;
    }

    public function hookHomePage($params)
    {
            global $smarty;

            $smarty->assign(
                            array(
                                    'link' => Configuration::get('youtube_link'),
                            )
                    );
            return $this->display(__FILE__, 'youtube.tpl');
    }

protected function addHook() {
            // Checking the module does not exist
            $exists = Db::getInstance()->getRow('
                            SELECT name
                            FROM '._DB_PREFIX_.'hook
                            WHERE name = "homepage"
                            ');
            // If it does not exist
            if (!$exists) {
                    $query = "INSERT INTO "._DB_PREFIX_."hook (`name`, `title`,
                    `description`) VALUES ('homepage', 'HomePage', 'Hooks in the
                    homepage');";
                    if(Db::getInstance()->Execute($query))
                            return true;
                    else
                            return false;
            }
            else return true;
    }

    public function getContent()
    {
            if (Tools::isSubmit('submit'))
            {
                    Configuration::updateValue('youtube_link', Tools::getValue
                    ('our_link'));
            }
            $this->displayForm();
            return $this->_html;
    }
```

```
private function displayForm()
{
        $this->_html .= '
        <form action="'.$_SERVER['REQUEST_URI'].'" method="post">
        <label>'.$this->l('YouTube video link').'</label>
        <div class="margin-form">
                <input type="text" name="our_link" />
        </div><br>
        <input type="submit" name="submit" value="'.$this->l('Save').'"
        class="button" />
        </form>';
}
}
```

The template file will add an iframe HTML tag where the $link Smarty variable will be used to set the link to our YouTube video (Listing 2-19).

Listing 2-19. Template File for YouTube Module

```
<div class="row">
        <h2> YouTube Video </h2>
        <iframe width="100%" height="500"
                src="{$link}">
        </iframe>
</div>
```

Now we can proceed with the installation of our YouTube module by clicking the Install button (Figure 2-17). Remember we didn't explicitly mention anything regarding the home page hook to which we are hooking our module, but be aware that you need to define where you'll put the $HOMEPAGE Smarty hook variable for linking the visual content to PrestaShop. In our case, we defined this variable in the index.tpl file, near the footer.

Figure 2-17. *YouTube module installed*

We set the link we want in the module's configuration page as illustrated in Figure 2-18.

Figure 2-18. *Setting YouTube link video on configuration page*

Finally, we can see our video being displayed on the home page.

■ **Note** If your module is attached to the top hook instead of the home page hook, you can always transplant it using Recipe 2-3 and moving it to the right place.

2-7. Configuring Your PS Site Using SQL Queries during Module Installation

Problem

You want to execute SQL queries in your module during its installation process.

Solution

To implement this behavior, we'll select any of the modules we have seen so far and modify their install() method. We'll also add a constant variable in the main PHP class to refer to an .sql file holding all of our queries.

How It Works

First, we create a constant variable by simply adding the next line as a class attribute:

```
const INSTALL_SQL_FILE = 'install.sql';
```

This variable will hold the name of the SQL file where all our queries will be contained; in this case, the file name is install.sql (Figure 2-19).

install.sql	6/29/2016 5:53 PM	SQL File	2 KB	
logo.gif	6/29/2016 5:53 PM	GIF image	43 KB	

Figure 2-19. *The SQL file must be at the same level as the logo*

The install.sql file contains a set of queries consisting of configurations to PS. The first statement creates a specific price rule named Deposit, the second sets the order process type as One Page Check Out, the third sets the registration process as only Account Creation, the forth allows ordering products out of stock, and the last one indicates PS to not display products quantities (Listing 2-20).

Listing 2-20. Configuration Queries in install.sql file

```
INSERT INTO `DBNAME_`.`PREFIX_specific_price_rule` (`id_specific_price_rule`, `name`,
`id_shop`, `id_currency`, `id_country`, `id_group`, `from_quantity`, `price`, `reduction`,
`reduction_type`, `from`, `to`)
VALUES (NULL, 'Deposit', '1', '0', '0', '0', '1', -1.00, '50.00', 'percentage', '', '');
UPDATE `DBNAME_`.`PREFIX_configuration` SET `value` = '1' WHERE `PREFIX_
configuration`.`name` = 'PS_ORDER_PROCESS_TYPE';
UPDATE `DBNAME_`.`PREFIX_configuration` SET `value` = '0' WHERE `PREFIX_
configuration`.`name` = 'PS_REGISTRATION_PROCESS_TYPE';
UPDATE `DBNAME_`.`PREFIX_configuration` SET `value` = '1' WHERE `PREFIX_
configuration`.`name` = 'PS_ORDER_OUT_OF_STOCK';
UPDATE `DBNAME_`.`PREFIX_configuration` SET `value` = '0' WHERE `PREFIX_
configuration`.`name` = 'PS_DISPLAY_QTIES';
UPDATE `DBNAME_`.`PREFIX_configuration` SET `value` = '0' WHERE `PREFIX_
configuration`.`name` = 'PS_CONDITIONS';
UPDATE `DBNAME_`.`PREFIX_configuration` SET `value` = '0' WHERE `PREFIX_
configuration`.`name` = 'PS_SHIPPING_HANDLING';
```

In this manner, we can configure PS without any real need to access the Back Office by simply surfing through the database and making the necessary alterations; evidently the Back Office is friendlier.

■ **Note** The, configuration object can also be used to configure your PrestaShop site. Variables can be accessed using the get method, in other words, Configuration::get('PS_SHOP_EMAIL') gives you the main contact e-mail address.

Finally, the install() method where the .sql file is loaded and all its queries executed is shown in Listing 2-21.

Listing 2-21. Install() Method

```
public function install()
    {
            if (!file_exists(dirname(__FILE__).'/'.self::INSTALL_SQL_FILE))
                return false;
            else if (!$sql = Tools::file_get_contents(dirname(__FILE__).'/'.
            self::INSTALL_SQL_FILE))
                return false;

            $sql = str_replace(array('PREFIX_',  'DBNAME_'), array
            (_DB_PREFIX_, _DB_NAME_), $sql);
            $sql = preg_split("/;\s*[\r\n]+/", $sql);

    foreach ($sql as $query) {
            if ($query) {
                    if (!Db::getInstance()->execute(trim($query)))
                    return false;
            }
    }

    if (!parent::install())
            return false;
            return true;
    }
```

The method starts by checking if the install.sql file exists in the module's root folder; if it does exist, it checks whether the file is not empty and puts its content in the $sql variable.

Every PREFIX_ or DBNAME_ string in the file is substituted by _DB_PREFIX_, _DB_NAME_ respectively in the $sql variable.

■ **Note**   The _DB_PREFIX_ variable refers to the PS database table prefix, usually ps and the _DB_NAME_ to the PS database name. These values can be defined in the settings.inc.php file located in the config folder at the PS package root.

We split the $sql string into different substrings using characters ("/;\s*[\r\n]+/") as separators. Lastly, every query is executed and, in the end, the parent's install method is called as it's the usual practice.

2-8. Module for Sending E-mail Notifications after Order Confirmation

Problem

You want to create a module that notifies you and others via e-mail when an order has been confirmed.

Solution

The solution we offer to this problem is to create an Order Email module that can be configured by adding the appropriate e-mail addresses as recipients and attach it to the displayOrderConfirmation hook.

How It Works

We'll start by duplicating the same module structure we have been recreating in this chapter (Figure 2-20).

Figure 2-20. *Module file structure*

The class name and its constructor can be seen in Listing 2-22.

Listing 2-22. Class Constructor

```
class OrderEmail extends Module {

        public function __construct()
        {
                $this->name = 'orderemail';
                $this->tab = 'emailing';
                $this->version = '1.0.0';
                $this->author = 'Arnaldo Perez Castano';
                $this->need_instance = 0;
                $this->ps_versions_compliancy = array('min' => '1.6', 'max' => _PS_VERSION_);
                $this->bootstrap = true;

                parent::__construct();

                $this->displayName = $this->l('Order Email');
                $this->description = $this->l('Send email notifications after order
                confirmation');

                $this->confirmUninstall = $this->l('Are you sure you want to uninstall?');
        }
```

Notice that in Listing 2-22 we changed the tab to which our module belongs in the Back Office; so far we have used front features and now we switched to e-mailing. Thus, the module will appear in the E-mailing & SMS section.

In the install() method, we now register to the displayOrderConfirmation hook (Listing 2-23).

Listing 2-23. Install Method

```
public function install()
{
            if (!parent::install() ||
                    !$this->registerHook('displayOrderConfirmation'))
                    return false;
            return true;
}
```

In order to configure our module, we implement the getContent() and displayForm() methods (Listing 2-24).

Listing 2-24. getContent() and displayForm() Methods

```
public function getContent()
        {
            if (Tools::isSubmit('submit'))
            {
                    Configuration::updateValue('emails', Tools::getValue('csv'));
            }
            $this->displayForm();
            return $this->_html;
        }

        private function displayForm()
        {
            $this->_html .= '
            <form action="'.$_SERVER['REQUEST_URI'].'" method="post">
            <label>'.$this->l('Email addresses to send notification email').'</label>
            <div class="margin-form">
                    <input type="text" name="csv" />
            </div><br>
            <input type="submit" name="submit" value="'.$this->l('Save').'"
            class="button" />
            </form>';
        }
```

We are proposing that the text field containing all e-mail addresses be a Comma Separated Values (CSV) type of string (for example, arnaldo.skywalker@gmail.com, michael@yahoo.com, and luis@gmx.com). By doing so, we make our module more general. To keep it simple, we will assume that only one e-mail address will be submitted via the Back Office; the generalization is left to the reader as exercise (Listing 2-25).

Listing 2-25. hookdisplayOrderConfirmation() Method

```
public function hookdisplayOrderConfirmation($params)
        {
            $email = Configuration::get('emails');
            mail ($email , 'New Order' , 'HCCT order');
        }
```

In the last method, we get the e-mail address saved in the module's configuration page and use the PHP mail function to send a message to $email with subject "New Order" and body "HCCT order".

■ **Note** If you would like to check the e-mail configuration of your PS site, follow the path Advanced Parameters->E-mail in the Back Office. There you can send a test e-mail to an address provided.

2-9. Adding More Information to Order E-mail Notifications

Problem

You want to add more information (total to be paid, customer name) on e-mail notifications that are received after order confirmations.

Solution

In the last recipe, we learned how to create a module that would notify us about order confirmations. Even though this could come in handy, in general you would like to receive more detailed information about the order that has been confirmed. The solution to offering a more detailed description lies on the $params input variable of the hookdisplayOrderConfirmation() method.

How It Works

So far, we have seen hooks methods without paying attention at the input variables that they incorporate. To get to know the contents of these variables, we need to look at the file where the hook is defined.

The displayOrderConfirmation hook, for instance, is defined in the OrderConfirmationController.php file located at /controllers/front/. At the end of the file, you can find the code from Listing 2-26.

Listing 2-26. displayOrderConfirmation() Method in OrderConfirmationController.php File

```
/**
    * Execute the hook displayOrderConfirmation
    */
    public function displayOrderConfirmation()
    {
        if (Validate::isUnsignedId($this->id_order)) {
            $params = array();
            $order = new Order($this->id_order);
            $currency = new Currency($order->id_currency);

            if (Validate::isLoadedObject($order)) {
                $params['total_to_pay'] = $order->getOrdersTotalPaid();
                $params['currency'] = $currency->sign;
                $params['objOrder'] = $order;
                $params['currencyObj'] = $currency;
```

```
                return Hook::exec('displayOrderConfirmation', $params);
        }
    }
    return false;
}
```

In the method, we can see the contents of the $params array variable being defined. For example, to get the total amount to be paid, we access $params['total_to_pay'], and to get the currency, we access $params['currency'].

There are two objects in place here, Order and Currency; their classes can be found in /classes/order and classes/ respectively.

The only adjustment we'll make to the Order E-mail module (created in the last recipe) will be in the hookdisplayOrderConfirmation() method. As you can see from Listing 2-27, the modification is quite simple—just change the message body to now show the total to be paid.

Listing 2-27. Modification on displayOrderConfirmation() Hook

```
public function hookdisplayOrderConfirmation($params)
    {
            $email = Configuration::get('emails');
            mail ($email , 'New Order' , 'HCCT order Total: '.$params['total_to_pay']);

    }
```

■ **Note** If you need to add more entries to the $params array, read through the Order and Currency classes to discover their methods and attributes and incorporate them by making the appropriate call. You should also override the OrderConfirmationController.php file to carry out this modification.

2-10. Changing CSS Styles through a Module

Problem

You want to change the CSS styles of your PrestaShop website in the Back Office without any need to interact directly with .css files.

Solution

The easiest solution to this problem is to install the CSS Editing module that you can find in the next link https://dh42.com/wp-content/uploads/2015/05/cssmodule.zip. Once you have installed (Figure 2-21) this free module, you can use it to edit any CSS styles of your PS site.

Figure 2-21. *CSS Editing module installed*

How It Works

Once you have downloaded and installed the module, click the Configure link and a text area will appear where you can define the styles of your store, as illustrated in Figure 2-22.

CSS Editing Module

```
Custom CSS :   body {
                   color: #666;
               }

               #paypal-express-checkout-btn-product, #paypal-express-checkout-form{
                       display: none;
               }

               .customizableProductsText {
                   margin-bottom: 0px;
                   padding-bottom: 0px;
                   border-bottom:none;
               }

               Save
```

Figure 2-22. *Editing styles*

Clicking the Save button finalizes the style definition process.

■ **Note**   Another option for editing your CSS styles is to edit the `globe.css` file located in the css folder of your current theme.

Summary

Throughout this chapter, we have presented several recipes for creating, positioning, and transplanting modules; we have described the creation of hooks and the creation of configuration pages for a module. We have also demonstrated how to create singular modules like the YouTube module. In the next chapter, we will examine recipes for customizing PrestaShop front-end features and providing a richer UI.

CHAPTER 3

Theme Development

Having a decent web design is something we all need in our web pages today; customers appreciate and are often captivated by a modern, refined, and elegant design. PrestaShop offers the possibility of changing your design through the use of themes.

A theme is basically a folder containing CSS, JS, images, and Smarty template files (those with .tpl extension) that, when put together, represent a certain web design. You can find themes oriented toward different types of businesses: clothing, fine art, publishing, automobiles, travel, and so on. PS allows you to choose the theme that fits your needs and products. Hence, if you are selling auto parts, you will probably go for an automobile theme. If you have a booking service, you might want to go for a travel theme.

In this chapter, we'll be examining various recipes for creating and customizing your PrestaShop themes. We'll explain the relation between PS theming and terms such as JQuery, AJAX, CSS, HTML, Smarty, and more. You will learn the following:

- How to create a PS theme

- How to create a welcome text in your PS home page

- How to set the image slider at full width

- How to add a datetimepicker to your product page

- How to save custom fields when clicking Add to Cart button

- How to change the font of your PS theme

- How to create a Testimonials module

- How to show a header in product page depending on product category

- How to customize e-mail templates

- How to add new variables to e-mail templates

- How to modify the Social Networking module to add a TripAdvisor link

- How to modify the MyAccount Footer module to display Links of Interest list.

- How to generate product attributes by adding product combinations

- How to associate attributes to products without combining

© Arnaldo Pérez Castaño 2017
A. P. Castaño, *PrestaShop Recipes*, DOI 10.1007/978-1-4842-2574-5_3

■ **Note**   PrestaShop uses the Smarty engine template to separate the visual part of the application (HTML, CSS, JS) from the logical part (PHP). In this manner, web designers can work independently on the Smarty, CSS, and JS files (`.tpl`, `.css`, and `.js` extensions, respectively) while web programmers work on the PHP files (`.php` extension).

3-1. How to Create a PS Theme

Problem

You want to create a custom layout/design for your PS site.

Solution

To create a custom layout or design, we need to create a custom theme. We can do it in the Back Office following the path `Preferences->Themes` (Figure 3-1).

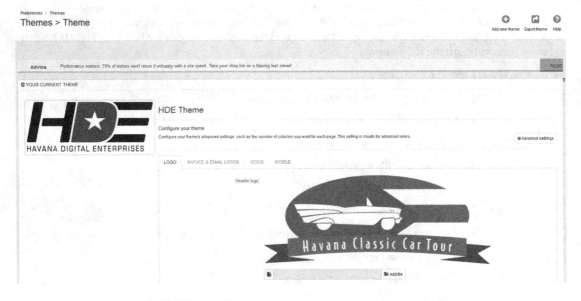

Figure 3-1. *Themes section in PS Back Office*

In the Themes section, we can select the header logo for our theme as well as the logos for e-mail, invoice, mobile version, and so forth. To create a new theme, we click the Add New Theme button in the upper right corner.

Then we'll be taken to a page where we can choose among various options to add a new theme to our PS site, as shown in Figure 3-2.

1. *Import from your computer*: It allows us to import a PS theme from our PC in the form of a `.zip` file.

2. *Import from the Web*: It is the same as the previous option but assumes the file is on the Web; you will need to indicate an URL, in this case, that ends in a `.zip` file.

3. *Import from FTP*: It assumes a `.zip` has been copied in the Themes folder of your PS package and allows you to select one.

4. *Create a new theme*: It duplicates an existing theme for later customization or allows you to create a new theme from scratch.

Preferences / Themes
Themes > Import theme

IMPORT FROM YOUR COMPUTER

Zip file   ▶   🗁 Add file

Browse your computer files and select the Zip file for your new theme.

IMPORT FROM THE WEB

Archive URL

Indicate the complete URL to an online Zip file that contains your new theme. For instance, "http://example.com/files/theme.zip".

IMPORT FROM FTP

Select the archive   -   ▾

This selector lists the Zip files that you uploaded in the '/themes' folder.

CREATE A NEW THEME

Duplicate an existing theme and edit it; or create a new theme from scratch! Recommended for advanced users only.

+ Create a new theme

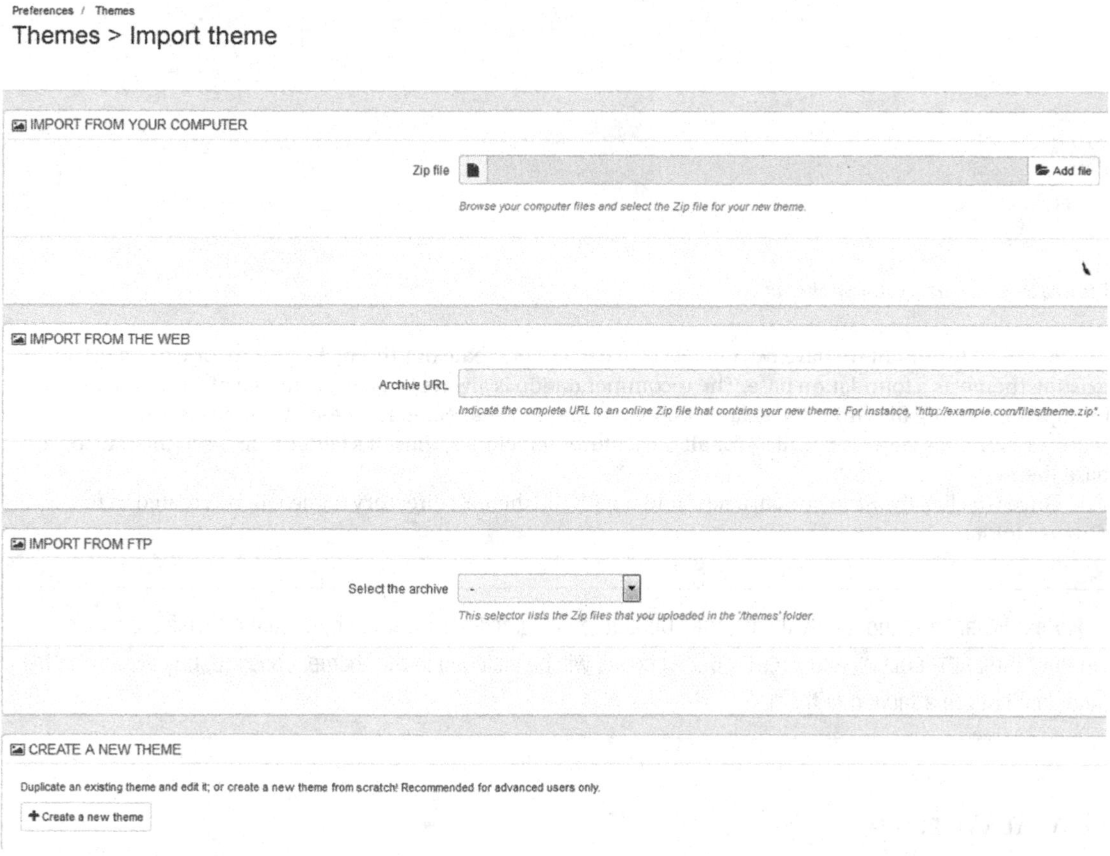

Figure 3-2. Various ways to incorporate a new theme to PS

We select the last option, which will permit us to create a new theme; this is illustrated in Figure 3-3.

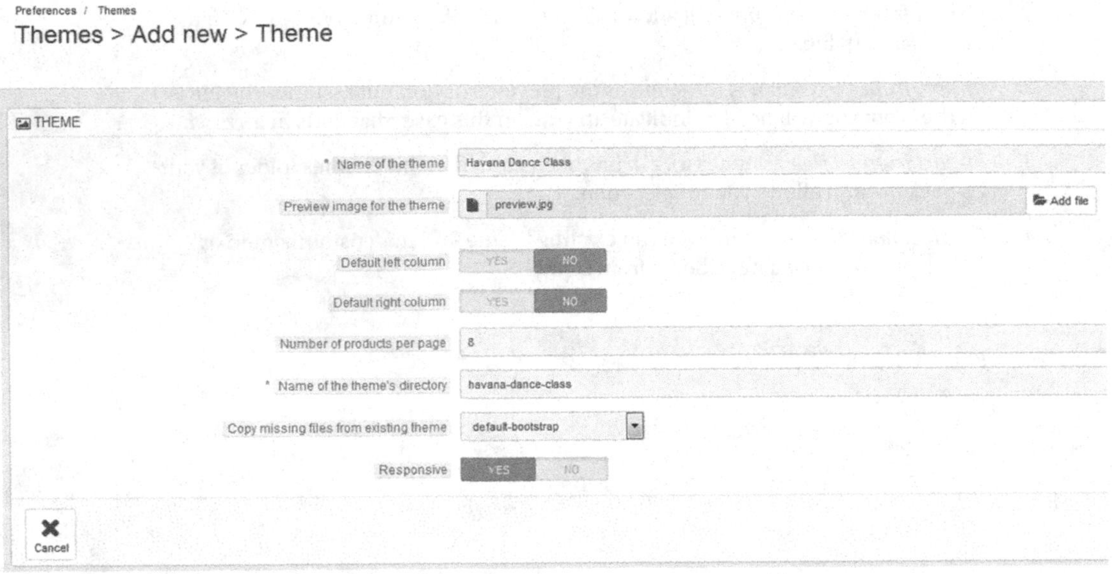

Preferences / Themes
Themes > Add new > Theme

Figure 3-3. *Creating a new theme*

Again, at this point we have two choices: We can either create our theme from zero, or we can use an existing theme as a foundation base. The recommendation is always to take advantage of a founding father by copying missing files from the default-bootstrap theme. PrestaShop is an e-commerce website and requires multiples views (.tpl files) for all the features it includes; thus, it's better to include them using a base theme.

Once we click the Save button, a new folder with the theme's directory name will be created in the Themes folder.

■ **Note**   When creating a new theme, the "Default left column" and "Default right column" fields indicate whether the LEFT_COLUMN and RIGHT_COLUMN hooks will be included in the theme, consequently displaying the modules that are attached to them.

How It Works

After creating the theme, we can go to the Themes folder at the root of our PS package and locate a folder with the theme's directory name (Figure 3-4).

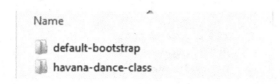

Figure 3-4. *Havana Dance Class theme in the Themes folder*

Even though we have created a new theme, PS still has the old theme set as the current for your shop; we need to update to the new one.

Under Preferences->Themes in the Back Office we can find, at the bottom, a list of available themes for your PS site, as shown in Figure 3-5.

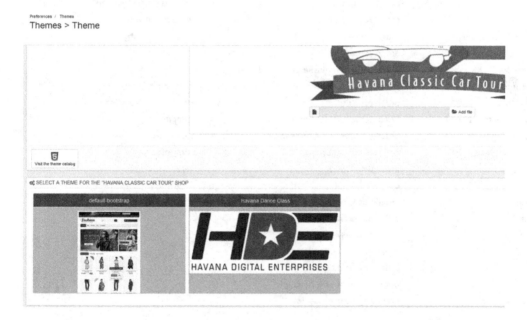

Figure 3-5. *Selecting your theme in PS Back Office*

To conclude, we set the one we just created (Havana Dance Class) by clicking the Use this Theme button, which appears when you pass the cursor over the theme's box. If you go to your FTP account and visit your themes folder, you will see the files of your new theme, as shown in Figure 3-6.

cache	header.tpl	order-return.tpl
css	history.tpl	order-slip.tpl
fonts	identity.tpl	order-steps.tpl
img	index.php	pagination.tpl
js	index.tpl	password.tpl
lang	layout.tpl	preview.jpg
mails	maintenance.tpl	prices-drop.tpl
mobile	manufacturer.tpl	product.tpl
modules	manufacturer-list.tpl	product-compare.tpl
pdf	my-account.tpl	product-list.tpl
sass	nbr-product-page.tpl	product-list-colors.tpl
404.tpl	new-products.tpl	products-comparison.tpl
address.tpl	order-address.tpl	product-sort.tpl
addresses.tpl	order-address-advanced.tpl	restricted-country.tpl
authentication.tpl	order-address-multishipping.tpl	scenes.tpl
best-sales.tpl	order-address-multishipping-products.tpl	search.tpl
breadcrumb.tpl	order-address-product-line.tpl	shopping-cart.tpl
category.tpl	order-carrier.tpl	shopping-cart-advanced.tpl
category-cms-tree-branch.tpl	order-carrier-advanced.tpl	shopping-cart-product-line.tpl
category-count.tpl	order-carrier-opc-advanced.tpl	sitemap.tpl
category-tree-branch.tpl	order-confirmation.tpl	store_infos.tpl
cms.tpl	order-detail.tpl	stores.tpl
config.rb	order-follow.tpl	supplier.tpl
config.xml	order-opc.tpl	supplier-list.tpl
contact-form.tpl	order-opc-advanced.tpl	
discount.tpl	order-opc-new-account.tpl	
errors.tpl	order-opc-new-account-advanced.tpl	
footer.tpl	order-payment.tpl	
global.tpl	order-payment-advanced.tpl	
guest-tracking.tpl	order-payment-classic.tpl	

Figure 3-6. *Files from the new theme Havana Dance Class*

■ **Note** The image that represents your theme is named `preview.jpg`, and you can overwrite it to change it; it's located at the root of your theme's folder.

3-2. Creating a Welcome Text in Your PS Home Page

Problem

You want to add a welcome message in your PS home page and perhaps also detail some of the benefits of buying or booking products and services through your website.

Solution

The template file (.tpl) that corresponds to our home page content is index.tpl, so first we need to find that file in our active theme (Figure 3-7).

history.tpl	6/29/2016 7:45 PM	TPL File	7 KB
identity.tpl	6/29/2016 7:45 PM	TPL File	11 KB
index.php	6/29/2016 7:45 PM	JetBrains PhpStorm	2 KB
index.tpl	1/2/2002 11:51 AM	TPL File	9 KB
layout.tpl	6/29/2016 7:45 PM	TPL File	2 KB
maintenance.tpl	6/29/2016 7:45 PM	TPL File	3 KB
manufacturer.tpl	6/29/2016 7:45 PM	TPL File	3 KB
manufacturer-list.tpl	6/29/2016 7:45 PM	TPL File	8 KB

Figure 3-7. Index.tpl file

Once we have located the template, we can edit it with any text editor. Notepad could do the trick.

How It Works

Inside index.tpl you will find a bunch of code that corresponds to the visual elements found between the header and footer. The content starts with the lines in Listing 3-1.

Listing 3-1. Refactoring the Directory Digest

```
{*
* 2007-2016 PrestaShop
*
* NOTICE OF LICENSE
*
* This source file is subject to the Academic Free License (AFL 3.0)
* that is bundled with this package in the file LICENSE.txt.
* It is also available through the world-wide-web at this URL:
* http://opensource.org/licenses/afl-3.0.php
* If you did not receive a copy of the license and are unable to
* obtain it through the world-wide-web, please send an email
* to license@prestashop.com so we can send you a copy immediately.
*
* DISCLAIMER
*
* Do not edit or add to this file if you wish to upgrade PrestaShop to newer
* versions in the future. If you wish to customize PrestaShop for your
* needs please refer to http://www.prestashop.com for more information.
*
*  @author PrestaShop SA <contact@prestashop.com>
*  @copyright  2007-2016 PrestaShop SA
*  @license    http://opensource.org/licenses/afl-3.0.php  Academic Free License (AFL 3.0)
*  International Registered Trademark & Property of PrestaShop SA
*}
```

In a Smarty template everything enclosed in {* ... *} are comments, meaning the text shown above is never displayed on the browser. Right below these comments we can write any HTML code that would represent the welcome, benefits section to be included.

```
<div class="row text-center">
        <h2 class="home-welcome">
                Welcome To Havana Classic Car Tours (HCCT)
        </h2>
        <h4 class="home-text">
        Today <span class="blue-text">Havana</span> is still a mysterious tropical paradise.
        More than 50 years of isolation from the rest of the world has forced the city to
        seem frozen in time. When people visit Havana they feel as if they have traveled
        back in time to the 40's or 50's. This marvellous journey will be unforgettable when
        you take a ride in a <span class="blue-text">Classic American Car</span>.
        <br><br>
        We will be instrumental in transporting you back in time for this once in a lifetime
        <span class="blue-text">AMAZING EXPERIENCE!!!</span>
                <br><br>
        </h4>
        <div class="content_scene_cat img-divisor"></div>
        <img alt="" src="{$img_dir}front-car.png" />
        <h4 class="home-text home-list">
        <img alt="" src="{$img_dir}icon/form-ok.png" />  We have predesigned <span
        class="blue-text">City Tours</span> created from our <span class="blue-text">Local
        Knowledge</span> of the city and it's most popular attractions. Our service can be
        flexible if you have something specific that you would like to add to your tour
        (additional charges may apply - ask your driver).
        </h4>
        <h4 class="home-text home-list">
<img alt="" src="{$img_dir}icon/form-ok.png" /> Pick up can be arranged at almost any place
in Havana, including hotels, private houses (Casa Particular), restaurants or paladars, just
<span class="blue-text">provide a specific and complete address</span> when booking your
tour.
        </h4>
        <h4 class="home-text home-list">
        <img alt="" src="{$img_dir}icon/form-ok.png" /> A <span class="blue-text">Guided
        Tour Service</span> in English is also available. Your driver is knowledgable and
        may offer a limited guide service in SPANGLISH, but he will be focused on driving
        and many details of the tour will be missed. Please select to add that service when
        booking your tour.
        </h4>
</div>
```

The previous code plus some CSS styles have the result shown in Figure 3-8 in our PS installation.

Welcome To Havana Classic Car Tours (HCCT)

Today Havana is still a mysterious tropical paradise. More than 50 years of isolation from the rest of the world has forced the city to seem frozen in time. When people visit Havana they feel as if they have traveled back in time to the 40's or 50's. This marvellous journey will be unforgettable when you take a ride in a Classic American Car.

We will be instrumental in transporting you back in time for this once in a lifetime AMAZING EXPERIENCE!!!

✔ We have predesigned City Tours created from our Local Knowledge of the city and it's most popular attractions. Our service can be flexible if you have something specific that you would like to add to your tour (additional charges may apply - ask your driver).

✔ Pick up can be arranged at almost any place in Havana, including hotels, private houses (Casa Particular), restaurants or paladars, just provide a specific and complete address when booking your tour.

✔ A Guided Tour Service in English is also available. Your driver is knowledgable and may offer a limited guide service in SPANGLISH, but he will be focused on driving and many details of the tour will be missed. Please select to add that service when booking your tour.

Figure 3-8. *Result of including welcome message in index.tpl file*

The `$img_dir` variable is a PrestaShop variable that indicates the path to the img folder in the active theme, that is, `ps_package/themes/your_theme_name/img/`.

■ **Note** Every content you add at the beginning of the `index.tpl` file will be displayed after the image slider and before the HomeFeatured module. That's a perfect spot for placing information sections about your business: welcome message, why book with us, and so on.

3-3. Image Slider at Full Width

Problem

You want to have the image slider on the home page shown at full width and not limited to a certain width, as it is PS default.

Solution

By default the image slider, which is a module, is not displayed at full width (Figure 3-9).

Figure 3-9. *Image slider in a fresh PS installation*

If we want to display the slider at 100% width, then a layout modification is required because the slider is contained within a div HTML element that restricts its width to a maximum width. We can inspect the page using our browser's inspector and check the default layout as shown in Figure 3-10.

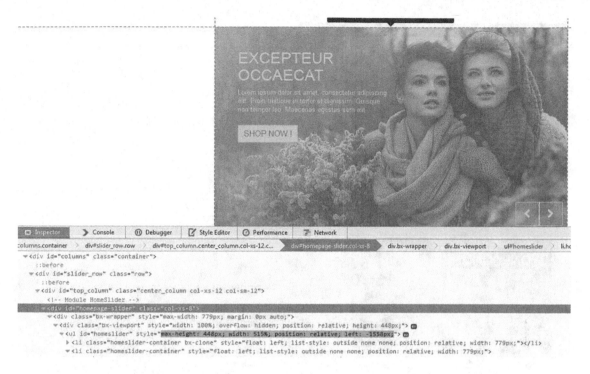

Figure 3-10. Inspecting PS home page in Mozilla Firefox by clicking Q button

---

■ **Note**   Most web browsers today provide developers tools for debugging and inspecting the code of your web pages. If we see the console shown in Figure 3-10, we'll noticed a max-width restriction imposed on a `div` HTML element.

How It Works

In order to set up the image slider at 100% width, we must get rid of the two images that are next to it. Therefore, we'll go to the Modules section in the PS Back Office, find the Theme Configurator module, and click its Configure button; we'll be taken to a page that contains Figure 3-11.

Figure 3-11. *Configuration page for Theme Configurator*

At the bottom of the configuration page, we'll see the two images attached to the Top hook. Simply delete them by clicking the Delete item in the drop-down box located in the right side of each image row.

Now we'll see the slider centered in the homepage (Figure 3-12) so the remaining tasks are to get it out of its enclosing div HTML element and make it wider.

Figure 3-12. *Slider centered*

If we inspect the code, we'll notice the div HTML element with id `top_column` as the immediate parent of another `div` with id `homepage_slider`, which is the container of our image slider. Now the first div (`top_column`) is enclosed in a third div element with id `slider_row`, as can be seen in Figure 3-13.

```
▼<div id="slider_row" class="row">
  ::before
  ▼<div id="top_column" class="center_column col-xs-12 col-sm-12">
    <!-- Module HomeSlider -->
  ▼<div id="homepage-slider" class="col-xs-12">
```

Figure 3-13. *Div element enclosing the slider*

This is the div element we'll need to find in the file `themes/your_theme/header.tpl`, as seen in Listing 3-2.

Listing 3-2. Fragment of header.tpl file

```
<div id="columns" class="container">
        {if $page_name !='index' && $page_name !='pagenotfound'}
        {include file="$tpl_dir./breadcrumb.tpl"}
        {/if}
        <div id="slider_row" class="row">
                <divid="top_column" class="center_column col-xs-12 col-sm-12">
{hook h="displayTopColumn"}
</div>
        </div>
```

We'll now take the slider_row div out of the columns div.

Listing 3-3. Moving Slider Div out of top_column Div

```
<div class="columns-container">
        <div id="slider_row" class="row">
                <div id="top_column" class="center_column col-xs-12 col-sm-12">{hook
                h="displayTopColumn"}</div>
        </div>
        <div id="columns" class="container">
                {if $page_name !='index' && $page_name !='pagenotfound'}
                {include file="$tpl_dir./breadcrumb.tpl"}
                {/if}
```

We now go back to the PS Back Office, find the Image Slider module, and click its Configure button. In the Settings section, we set the Max Width field to zero and save it. This will indicate that we don't want to have a max width for the slider (Figure 3-14).

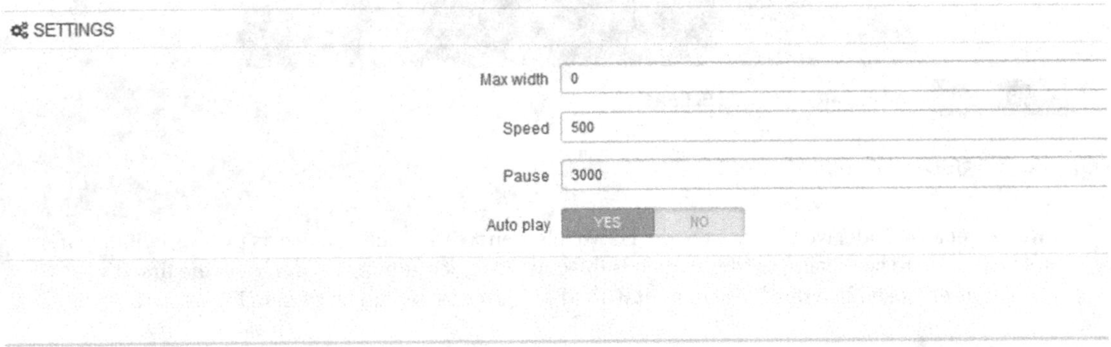

Figure 3-14. Setting max width to zero

Finally, we delete all PS default images and replace them with images of a really big width; making the image occupy the full width is recommended to avoid having to mess with the width and height properties of the img HTML tag itself and preventing the loose of the appropriate image proportions (Figure 3-15).

Figure 3-15. *Image slider at full width*

In the configuration page of the Image Slider module, you can now adjust transition speed according to your needs.

3-4. Adding a Datetimepicker to Your Product Page

Problem

You need a datetimepicker field on your product page to specify delivery or booking service date/time.

Solution

In order to solve this problem, we'll incorporate a JQuery calendar to our PS product page to give customers the possibility of selecting the date/time of their service (Figure 3-16).

Figure 3-16. JQuery datetimepicker

PrestaShop includes a date/time picker that uses different pages in the Back Office. You can find it by going to the Stats section and clicking the From or To textbox fields, as shown in Figure 3-17. To simplify the task, we'll reuse this calendar to solve our problem.

Figure 3-17. Datetimepicker in Stats section

The solution can be discomposed in three main parts. First, we need to define a text field that will act as container of the date/time specified. Second, we include the necessary scripts and style sheets links in the product page for the datetimepicker to work. Lastly, we include in the product.tpl file a script that makes the datetimepicker functional.

How It Works

The first part of the solution will consist in adding a Customization field for the product page that requires a date specification. For this purpose, we visit the PS Back Office, follow the path Catalog->Products, select the product we want to add (the date field), and click its Customization tab, as illustrated in Figure 3-18.

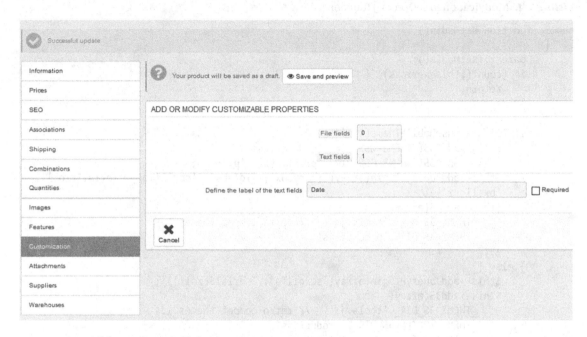

Figure 3-18. *Adding custom field date*

There we create a text field labeled Date (or any other label you may find appropriate) and click the Save button. If we now visit the product page, we'll notice a new Product Customization section (Figure 3-19).

PRODUCT CUSTOMIZATION

After saving your customized product, remember to add it to your cart.

Text
Date

Save

* required fields

Figure 3-19. *Product Customization on product page*

Once we have created the container for the datetimepicker, we need to add links to every necessary CSS and JS files in the product.tpl header. In order to complete this task, we'll copy the ProductController.php file located in /controllers/front and paste it in override/controllers/front. Let's edit the setMedia() function on the ProductController.php file we just copied and pasted, as seen in Listing 3-4.

Listing 3-4. Modification to setMedia() function

```php
public function setMedia()
    {
        parent::setMedia();
        if (count($this->errors)) {
            return;
        }

        if (!$this->useMobileTheme()) {
            $this->addCSS(_THEME_CSS_DIR_.'product.css');
            $this->addCSS(_THEME_CSS_DIR_.'print.css', 'print');
            $this->addJqueryPlugin(array('fancybox', 'idTabs', 'scrollTo', 'serialScroll',
            'bxslider'));
            $this->addJS(array(
                _THEME_JS_DIR_.'tools.js',  // retro compat themes 1.5
                _THEME_JS_DIR_.'product.js'
            ));
        } else {
            $this->addJqueryPlugin(array('scrollTo', 'serialScroll'));
            $this->addJS(array(
                _THEME_JS_DIR_.'tools.js',  // retro compat themes 1.5
                _THEME_MOBILE_JS_DIR_.'product.js',
                _THEME_MOBILE_JS_DIR_.'jquery.touch-gallery.js'
            ));
        }

if (Configuration::get('PS_DISPLAY_JQZOOM') == 1) {
            $this->addJqueryPlugin('jqzoom');
        }

        // New lines where links to CSS, JS files are added.
            $this->addCSS(array(_PS_JS_DIR_.'jquery/plugins/timepicker/jquery-ui-
            timepicker-addon.css'));

            $this->addJqueryUI(array(
                    'ui.widget',
                    'ui.slider',
                    'ui.datepicker'
            ));

            $this->addJS(array(
                    _PS_JS_DIR_.'jquery/plugins/timepicker/jquery-ui-timepicker-addon.js',
            ));
    }
```

The last lines added to the function represent the modification and add the necessary links to CSS and JS files.

■ **Note** The addCSS() and addJS() functions, respectively, add CSS and JS files to the page header. The addJqueryUI() does the same but adds scripts from a specific folder in the PS package (js/jquery/ui).

Even though we created a container for the datepicker in product.tpl, that container is by default a textarea HTML element and we need it to be an input element. Thus, we delete the textarea element shown in Listing 3-5.

Listing 3-5. Fragment of Code Belonging to product.tpl

```
<ul id="text_fields">
        {counter start=0 assign='customizationField'}
        {foreach from=$customizationFields item='field' name='customizationFields'}
            {if $field.type == 1}
                    <li class="customizationUploadLine{if $field.required}
                    required{/if}">
                    <label for ="textField{$customizationField}">
                            {assign var='key' value='textFields_'|cat:$product-
>id|cat:'_'|cat:$field.id_customization_field}
                                {if !empty($field.name)}
                                        {$field.name}
                                {/if}
                                {if $field.required}<sup>*</sup>{/if}
                    </label>
                    <textarea name="textField{$field.id_customization_field}"
                    class="form-control customization_block_input"
                    id="textField{$customizationField}" rows="3" cols="20">
{strip}
                        {if isset($textFields.$key)}
                                {$textFields.$key|stripslashes}
                        {/if}
                {/strip}</textarea>
            </li>
            {counter}
{/if}
{/foreach}
</ul>
```

In its place, we put the input element shown in Listing 3-6.

Listing 3-6. Input Element Replacing Textarea Element in product.tpl File

```
<input type="text" name="textField{$field.id_customization_field}" class="custom_datepicker
form-control customization_block_input" id="textField{$customizationField}"

            value="{if isset($textFields.$key)}{$textFields.$key|stripslashes}{/if}" >
```

Note that we defined the `custom_datepicker` class in the input; we'll need it for the last part of our solution, which consists of writing the JavaScript code for activating the datepicker. This code can be inserted after the closing (`</ul>`) list element in Listing 3-6. (See Listing 3-7.)

Listing 3-7. Script to Activate datepicker

```javascript
<script type="text/javascript">

        $(document).ready( function() {

                    $('.custom_datepicker').datepicker({

                            prevText: '',

                            nextText: '',

                            dateFormat: 'yy-mm-dd',

                            firstDay:0,

                            currentText: 'Now',

                            closeText: 'Done',

                            constrainInput: true

                    });
});
        </script>
```

Finally, we can see our datepicker in action by clicking the input element previously added as can be seen in Figure 3-20.

Figure 3-20. *Datepicker displayed*

If you want to include a timepicker, all you have to do is change the `datepicker` function in the script to `datetimepicker`. (See Listing 3-8.)

Listing 3-8. Changing Function Signature to datetimepicker

```
$('.custom_datepicker').datetimepicker({
```

Now the resulting calendar (Figure 3-21) will include date and time specified in hours and minutes.

Figure 3-21. *Datetimepicker displayed*

The datepicker included in PS has many options that allow you to customize the control. In Listing 3-7, we can see some of these options. The dateformat option, for instance, gives you the possibility of specifying the format you want for your date. firstday indicates the day you want to display as the first day of the week, being Sunday number 0. You can explore these options in the URL https://jqueryui.com/datepicker and adjust your datepicker to your needs.

■ **Note**   To save custom fields values, you must click the Save button located at the bottom of the Product Customization section.

3-5. Saving Custom Fields When Clicking the Add to Cart Button

Problem

You want to save custom field values when a customer clicks the Add to Cart button instead of having the middle step of saving them first.

Solution

To solve this problem, we need to modify several PS files whose code represents part of the "Add to cart" operation. The first file we need to modify is themes/your_theme/js/modules/blockcart/ajax-cart.js, a JavaScript file that handles all the AJAX-cart-related mechanisms you see when you interact with the page. We need to modify it in order to get the value from the front end (product.tpl) sent to the back end. In a second step, we would need to modify the override/controllers/front/ProductController.php file so it can receive data sent by the AJAX file and handle its processing; this is the back-end component.

How It Works

First, we'll add some lines to the code in Listing 3-9, located in ajax-cart.js file, near line 280.

Listing 3-9. Fragment of Function That Handles Product Addition to Cart

```
// add a product in the cart via ajax
add : function(idProduct, idCombination, addedFromProductPage, callerElement, quantity,
whishlist){

            if (addedFromProductPage && !checkCustomizations())
            {
                if (contentOnly)
                {
                    var productUrl = window.document.location.href + '';
                    var data = productUrl.replace('content_only=1', '');
                    window.parent.document.location.href = data;
                    return;
                }
```

```
                          if (!!$.prototype.fancybox)
                              $.fancybox.open([
                                  {
                                            type: 'inline',
                                            autoScale: true,
                                            minHeight: 30,
                                            content: '<p class="fancybox-error">' +
                                            fieldRequired + '</p>'
                                  }
                              ], {
                                      padding: 0
                              });
                          else
                                  alert(fieldRequired);
                          return;
                  }
```

The lines of code in Listing 3-9 correspond to a JS function that is executed when you click the Add to Cart button and only if you have the AJAX mode available in the cart module configuration. Before the first if statement, we'll insert the next code shown in Listing 3-10.

Listing 3-10. Code to Be Inserted

```
// Product Box Custom Form
$('#quantityBackup').val($('#quantity_wanted').val());
customAction = $('#customizationForm').attr('action');
$('body select[id^="group_"]').each(function() {
              customAction = customAction.replace(new RegExp(this.id + '=\\d+'),
              this.id +'=' + this.value);
});

// ajax to product page with custom action
var customization_entries = $('#customizationForm').serialize();
$.ajax({
              async:false,
              type: 'POST',
              data: customization_entries+ '&ajax=1',
              dataType: 'json',
              url: customAction,
              success: function(data){
              if(typeof(data.errors) !== 'undefined'){
                      alert('Error while saving customization data');
                      return;
              }
      }
})
```

In the first part of this code, we capture the URL defined in the action attribute of the customization form "#customizationForm" (the one containing our custom fields) and add the id/value pair of every field in the product box as part of it. In the second part, we post the URL with all necessary data as defined in customization_entries (serialization of the customization form) to a method in the ProductController for further processing. Now we add the function in Listing 3-11 to the override of the `ProductControllerCore` class located in the `ProductController.php` file.

Listing 3-11. Function to Be Inserted in ProductControllerCore Class

```
public function postProcess()
    {
            if (Tools::getValue('ajax') && Tools::isSubmit('submitCustomizedDatas'))
            {
// If cart has not been saved, we need to do it so that customization fields can have an
id_cart
                // We check that the cookie exists first to avoid ghost carts
                    if (!$this->context->cart->id && isset($_COOKIE[$this->
                    context->cookie->getName()]))
                    {
                            $this->context->cart->add();
                            $this->context->cookie->id_cart = (int)$this->context->cart->id;
                    }

                    $this->pictureUpload();
                    $this->textRecord();
                    $this->formTargetFormat();

                    if($this->errors)
                    {
                            $error_list = implode('; ', $this->errors);
                            die(Tools::jsonEncode(array('errors' => $error_list)));
                    } else
                            die(Tools::jsonEncode(array('success' => true)));

            }
    }
```

The built-in method `postProcess()` handles post data in PS. We start by checking that the form posted refers to a customization form being saved; such checking is accomplished by verifying the form is submitted via a "submitCustomizedDatas" button. We also check that it corresponds to an AJAX call. The block of code within the outer `if` statement is exactly the code PS uses when submitting a regular customization form, and you can find it in `ProductController.php` at the `initContent()` method. We move to the Summary page to see that everything went well (Figure 3-22).

SHOPPING-CART SUMMARY

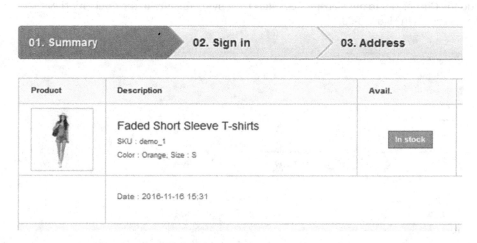

Figure 3-22. *Custom date field added to product description*

After defining a date in the product page and clicking the Save button, we'll see that the custom field is saved and added to the product's description in the cart, which completes this recipe.

■ **Note**   Serialization relates to the process of encoding data structures or objects into strings or other formats that can be stored on a file or transmitted through network connections and later reconstructed in the same or another environment.

3-6. Changing the Font of Your PS Theme

Problem

You want to change the font of your PS theme.

Solution

In the web world, fonts are commonly added to web pages via CSS rules. To solve this problem we'll first copy the files that correspond to our fonts in themes/your_theme/fonts/. Then we'll link this font to the site using CSS rules and the CSS Editing module presented in Chapter 2.

How It Works

In this case, we'll add the Corbel font to our website. Let's start by copying the files to the directory `themes/your_theme/fonts/`, as shown in Figure 3-23.

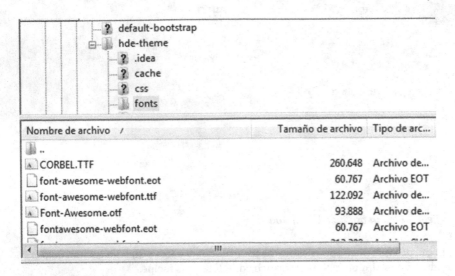

Figure 3-23. *Corbel font files*

Now that we have the font files in place, we just need to link them to our website. For that purpose, we'll go to the Back Office, visit the Modules and Services section, and locate the CSS Editing Module. Then we'll add the lines in Listing 3-12. The result can be seen in Figure 3-24.

Listing 3-12. Font Added Using CSS Rule

```
@font-face {
  font-family: 'Corbel';
src: url("your_domain/themes/your_theme/fonts/CORBEL.TTF");
}
```

Figure 3-24. *Corbel font being used in top menu*

In this case, we are using an absolute path to the font file, but we can also use a relative path if we define the same rule in the file themes/your_theme/css/global.css. In that case, the URL will change to url("../fonts/CORBEL.TTF").

3-7. Testimonials Module

Problem

You want to include customer testimonials in your home page and be able to configure them through a PS module.

Solution

In order to solve this problem, we'll create a module that encompasses all testimonials functionalities, that is, setting name, text, and image of a testimony (Figure 3-25).

config.xml

logo.png

testimonials.css

testimonials.php

testimonials.tpl

Figure 3-25. *Files from Testimonials module*

To get a quick start, we will copy and paste the YouTube module we created in Chapter 2 and change the name of its folder to "testimonials" and also the name of the .tpl and .php files.

How It Works

Let's start with the testimonials.php file where we'll define the different methods for configuring our module. Furthermore, we'll define a new hook named testimonials and set it up on the home page. In the code in Listing 3-13, we can see the beginning of the Testimonials class and its constructor.

Listing 3-13. Constructor Testimonials Class

```
class Testimonials extends Module {

    public function __construct()
{

            $this->name = 'testimonials';
            $this->tab = 'front_office_features';
            $this->version = '1.0.0';
            $this->author = 'Arnaldo Perez Castano';
            $this->need_instance = 0;
            $this->ps_versions_compliancy = array('min' => '1.6', 'max' => _PS_VERSION_);
            $this->bootstrap = true;

            parent::__construct();

            $this->displayName = $this->l('Testimonials');
            $this->description = $this->l('Display testimonials on homepage');

            $this->confirmUninstall = $this->l('Are you sure you want to uninstall?');
    }
```

This module constructor is basically what we have seen so far—information details of your module. Now, to register and add a new hook to PS database we incorporate the install() and addHook() functions to the class, as shown in Listing 3-14.

Listing 3-14. Adding and Registering the testimonials Hook

```
public function install()
        {
                if (!parent::install() ||
                        !$this->registerHook('testimonials'))
                        return false;
                return true;
        }

public function uninstall()
        {
                if (!parent::uninstall())
                        return false;
                return true;
        }

        protected function addHook()
        {
                // Checking the module does not exist
                $exists = Db::getInstance()->getRow('
                        SELECT name
                        FROM '._DB_PREFIX_.'hook
                        WHERE name = "testimonials"
                        ');
                // If it does not exist
                if (!$exists) {
                        $query = "INSERT INTO "._DB_PREFIX_."hook (`name`, `title`,
                        `description`) VALUES ('testimonials', 'Testimonials',
                        'Hooks in the homepage');";
                        if(Db::getInstance()->Execute($query))
                                return true;
                        else
                                return false;
                }
                else return true;
        }
```

Once we install the module, the new testimonials hook will be added to the database, so it's time to define the hookTestimonials() method. (Listing 3-15)

Listing 3-15. Adding and Registering the testimonials Hook

```
public function hookTestimonials($params)
        {
                global $smarty;
                // Set path to testimonials.css file
                Tools::addCSS($this->_path.'testimonials.css', 'all');
```

```
$smarty->assign(
            array(
                    'testimonial_1' => Configuration::get('testimonial_1'),
                    'testimonial_2' => Configuration::get('testimonial_2'),
                    'testimonial_3' => Configuration::get('testimonial_3'),
                'name_1' => Configuration::get('name_1'),
                'name_2' => Configuration::get('name_2'),
                'name_3' => Configuration::get('name_3'),
                'image_1' => Configuration::get('image_1'),
                'image_2' => Configuration::get('image_2'),
                'image_3' => Configuration::get('image_3'),
            )
        );

        return $this->display(__FILE__, 'testimonials.tpl');
    }
```

Again we are using the PS Configuration object to save variables related to configuration issues. Every Smarty variable refers to a given testimonial. Thus, we will have a total of three testimonials all set in one row, and they will include a name, testimony, and image.

In order to customize our three testimonials, we will add a Configure link to the module. As we know from Chapter 2, this can be achieved by developing the getContent() method. (Listing 3-16)

Listing 3-16. getContent() and displayForm() Methods

```
public function getContent()
    {
            if (Tools::isSubmit('submit'))
            {
                    Configuration::updateValue('testimonial_1', Tools::getValue('testim
                    onial_1'));
                    Configuration::updateValue('testimonial_2', Tools::getValue('testim
                    onial_2'));
                    Configuration::updateValue('testimonial_3', Tools::getValue('testim
                    onial_3'));
                    Configuration::updateValue('name_1', Tools::getValue('name_1'));
                    Configuration::updateValue('name_2', Tools::getValue('name_2'));
                    Configuration::updateValue('name_3', Tools::getValue('name_3'));

                    $image_1 = $_FILES['image_1'];
                    $image_2 = $_FILES['image_2'];
                    $image_3 = $_FILES['image_3'];

            $this->imageCheck($image_1);
                    $this->imageCheck($image_2);
                    $this->imageCheck($image_3);

                    Configuration::updateValue('image_1', $_FILES['image_1']['name']);
                    Configuration::updateValue('image_2', $_FILES['image_2']['name']);
                    Configuration::updateValue('image_3', $_FILES['image_3']['name']);
            }
```

```
            $this->displayForm();
            return $this->_html;
    }

    private function displayForm()
{
            $this->_html .= '
            <form action="'.$_SERVER['REQUEST_URI'].'" method="post"
            enctype="multipart/form-data">
            <label>'.$this->l('Testimonial #1').'</label>
            <div class="margin-form">
                    <textarea name="testimonial_1"></textarea>
            </div><br>
            <label>'.$this->l('Name #1').'</label>
            <div class="margin-form">
                    <input type="text" name="name_1" />
                    <input type="file" name="image_1" />
            </div>
            <br>
            <div class="margin-form">
                    <textarea name="testimonial_2"></textarea>
            </div><br>
            <label>'.$this->l('Name #2').'</label>
            <div class="margin-form">
                    <input type="text" name="name_2" />
                    <input type="file" name="image_2" />
            </div>
            <br>
            <div class="margin-form">
                    <textarea name="testimonial_3"></textarea>
            </div><br>
            <label>'.$this->l('Name #3').'</label>
            <div class="margin-form">
                    <input type="text" name="name_3" />
                    <input type="file" name="image_3" />
            </div>
            <br>
            <input type="submit" name="submit" value="'.$this->l('Save').'"
            class="button" />
            </form>';
}
```

The displayForm() method will contain the form being displayed after clicking the Configure link. Once this form is submitted, the getContent() method will save each name, testimony text using the Configuration object and it will also save the specified image on the upload folder at PS root.

■ **Note**   The configuration form of the Testimonials module must include the `enctype="multipart/form-data"` attribute to allow saving files when submitting data. The `$_FILES` variable contains every file submitted and can be accessed by means of indexing.

The function where images are saved is imageCheck(). (Listing 3-17)

Listing 3-17. imageCheck() Method

```php
private function imageCheck($image)
        {
        //Check the image exists
if ($image['name'] != "" )
{
// Allowed image formats
$allowed = array('image/gif', 'image/jpeg', 'image/jpg', 'image/png');

// Verify the image has a valid format
if (in_array($image['type'], $allowed))
{
$path = '../upload/';

// Check the image does not exist already
 if(!move_uploaded_file($image['tmp_name'], $path.$image['name']) )
{
$output .= $this->displayError( $path.$image['name'] );
return $output.$this->displayForm();
}
}
else
        {
                $output .= $this->displayError( $this->l('Invalid image format.') );
                return $output.$this->displayForm();
        }
    }
    }
```

In the imageCheck() function, we first check that the image object supplied as argument is not empty. Later, we check that the image format is one of the allowed formats (JPG, JPEG, PNG). Finally, we save the image to the upload folder and, in case there's a problem during the previous operations, an error message is displayed.

A final step is required to make our Testimonials module visible. Remember it's attached to a hook that we created that is not part of the PS native hooks, so we need to define a place for the $HOOK_TESTIMONIALS variable. In our case, that place will be on the home page. Therefore, we'll edit the index.tpl file in the current theme and add {$HOOK_TESTIMONIALS}.

Another task is still pending; we need to associate the $HOOK_TESTIMONIALS variable with the value resulting of the hook's execution. This can be done in the IndexController.php file. We'll create an override (copy and paste original file to override/controllers/front/) and edit the initContent() method as shown in Listing 3-18.

Listing 3-18. Adding HOOK_TESTIMONIALS Smarty Variable

```
public function initContent()
    {
        parent::initContent();
        $this->addJS(_THEME_JS_DIR_.'index.js');

        $this->context->smarty->assign(array('HOOK_HOME' => Hook::exec('displayHome'),
            'HOOK_HOME_TAB' => Hook::exec('displayHomeTab'),
            'HOOK_HOME_TAB_CONTENT' => Hook::exec('displayHomeTabContent'),
         'HOOK_TESTIMONIALS' => Hook::exec('testimonials')
        ));
        $this->setTemplate(_PS_THEME_DIR_.'index.tpl');
    }
```

To conclude, let us install the module (Figure 3-26).

Figure 3-26. *Testimonial module installed*

Click the Configure link and start defining some testimonials, as illustrated in Figure 3-27.

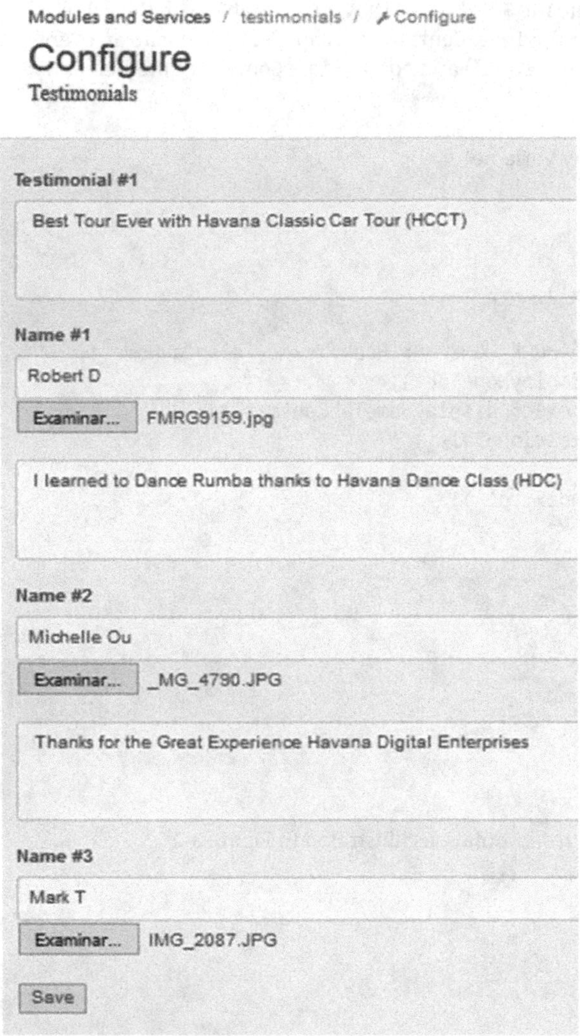

Modules and Services / testimonials / Configure
Configure
Testimonials
Testimonial #1
Best Tour Ever with Havana Classic Car Tour (HCCT)
Name #1
Robert D
Examinar...
FMRG9159.jpg
I learned to Dance Rumba thanks to Havana Dance Class (HDC)
Name #2
Michelle Ou
Examinar...
_MG_4790.JPG
Thanks for the Great Experience Havana Digital Enterprises
Name #3
Mark T
Examinar...
IMG_2087.JPG
Save

Figure 3-27. *Defining new testimonials*

After clicking the Save button, we'll be able to see the result on the home page where we defined the `$HOOK_TESTIMONIALS` variable (Figure 3-28).

Best Tour Ever with Havana Classic Car Tour (HCCT)
Robert D
I learned to Dance Rumba thanks to Havana Dance Class (HDC)
Michelle Ou
Thanks for the Great Experience Havana Digital Enterprises
Mark T

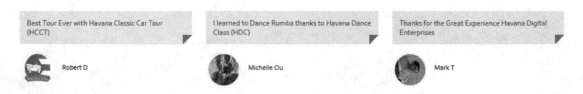

Figure 3-28. *Testimonials in PS home page*

If you are curious about the template or CSS files, these are presented in Listing 3-19.

Listing 3-19. Contents of testimonials.tpl File

```
<div class="row">
<div class="col-md-4">
<div class="testimonials">
        <div class="active item">
<blockquote><p>{$testimonial_1}</p></blockquote>
<div class="carousel-info">
<img alt="" src="{$pic_dir}/{$image_1}" class="pull-left">
<div class="pull-left">
<span class="testimonials-name">{$name_1}</span>
<span class="testimonials-post"></span>
</div>
</div>
</div>
</div>
</div>
                <div class="col-md-4">
<div class="testimonials">
        <div class="active item">
<blockquote><p>{$testimonial_2}</p></blockquote>
<div class="carousel-info">
<img alt="" src="{$pic_dir}/{$image_2}" class="pull-left">
<div class="pull-left">
<span class="testimonials-name">{$name_2}</span>
<span class="testimonials-post"></span>
</div>
</div>
</div>
</div>
</div>
                <div class="col-md-4">
<div class="testimonials">
        <div class="active item">
<blockquote><p>{$testimonial_3}</p></blockquote>
<div class="carousel-info">
<img alt="" src="{$pic_dir}/{$image_3}" class="pull-left">
<div class="pull-left">
<span class="testimonials-name">{$name_3}</span>
<span class="testimonials-post"></span>
</div>
</div>
</div>
</div>
</div>
</div>
```

The testimonials.css file would contain the lines in Listing 3-20.

Listing 3-20. Contents of testimonials.css File

```css
.testimonials blockquote {
    background: #D9EFF2 none repeat scroll 0 0;
    border: medium none;
    color: #666;
    display: block;
    font-size: 14px;
    line-height: 20px;
    padding: 15px;
    position: relative;
}
.testimonials blockquote::before {
    width: 0;
    height: 0;
        right: 0;
        bottom: 0;
        content: " ";
        display: block;
        position: absolute;
    border-bottom: 20px solid #fff;
        border-right: 0 solid transparent;
        border-left: 15px solid transparent;
        border-left-style: inset; /*FF fixes*/
        border-bottom-style: inset; /*FF fixes*/
}
.testimonials blockquote::after {
    width: 0;
    height: 0;
    right: 0;
    bottom: 0;
    content: " ";
    display: block;
position: absolute;
    border-style: solid;
border-width: 20px 20px 0 0;
    border-color: #0F83B9 transparent transparent transparent;
}
.testimonials .carousel-info img {
border: 1px solid #f5f5f5;
    border-radius: 150px !important;
height: 75px;
    padding: 3px;
    width: 75px;
}
.testimonials .carousel-info {
    overflow: hidden;
}
```

```
.testimonials .carousel-info img {
    margin-right: 15px;
}
.testimonials .carousel-info span {
    display: block;
}
.testimonials span.testimonials-name {
font-size: 15px;
    font-weight: 500;
margin: 23px 0px 7px;
    color: #012;
}
.testimonials span.testimonials-post {
    color: #656565;
    font-size: 12px;
}
```

Now that you have all the elements for creating a Testimonials module, you can go ahead and customize it to your needs, perhaps adding a fourth testimonial or changing its layout or styles.

3-8. Showing a Header in Product Page Depending on Product Category

Problem

You want to show different header texts depending on the product category.

Solution

To solve this problem, we'll edit the product.tpl file where the product header is displayed and add the necessary logic to control whether one text or the other will be shown depending on product category.

How It Works

In the product.tpl file of your active theme, locate a div HTML element with class page-product-heading and edit its contents as shown in Listing 3-21.

Listing 3-21. Fragment of Modified product.tpl File

```
<h3 class="page-product-heading">
        {if $product->category == 'tours'}
                {l s='TOUR DETAILS'}
        {else}
                {l s='DETAILS'}
        {/if}
</h3>
```

Using the category attribute of the product object, we can know the category of the current product. Thus, applying a simple 'if' logic in Smarty language, we can display one text or the other depending on the value of the previously mentioned attribute (Figure 3-29).

Figure 3-29. *Product header text according to product category*

In case you have more than two independents categories, you can create a Smarty if statement with multiples {elseif} clauses within its body, that is, between {if} ... {/if} and controlling the logic for different categories and texts associated.

3-9. Customizing E-mail Templates

Problem

You want to customize your e-mail templates to show new data.

Solution

In order to customize e-mail templates, we need to go to PS Back Office and follow the path Localization-> Translations, as shown in Figure 3-30.

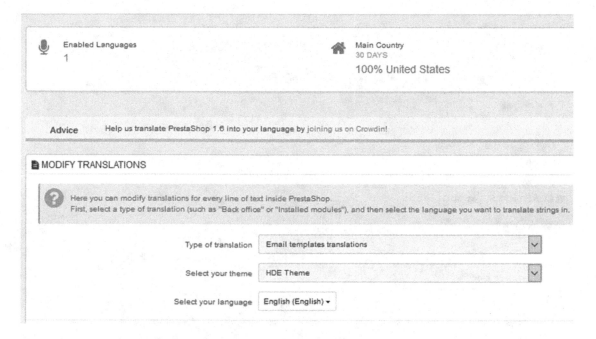

Figure 3-30. *Translations page in PS Back Office*

After selecting "Email templates translations," your current theme, and language, click the Modify button and a list of all e-mail templates will appear.

How It Works

Once in the e-mail templates page, click Core Emails and a list of the most important templates will show up, as seen in Figure 3-31.

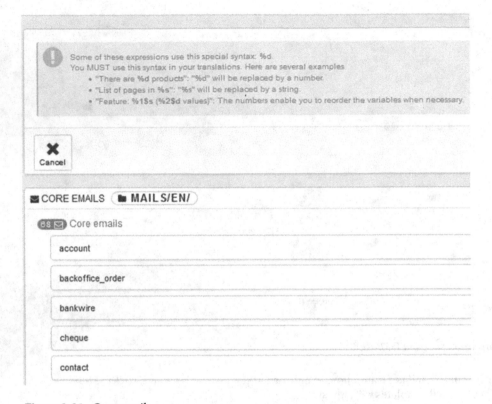

Localization / Translations

Translations

Some of these expressions use this special syntax: %d.
You MUST use this syntax in your translations. Here are several examples
- "There are %d products": "%d" will be replaced by a number.
- "List of pages in %s": "%s" will be replaced by a string.
- "Feature: %1$s (%2$d values)": The numbers enable you to reorder the variables when necessary.

✖
Cancel

✉ CORE EMAILS   (🗀 MAILS/EN/)

68 ✉ Core emails

account

backoffice_order

bankwire

cheque

contact

Figure 3-31. *Core emails*

If we now click the account link and edit the HTML version, we'll see that we can easily change text, insert image and links, or add and remove columns and rows by executing a right-click the edition panel (Figure 3-32).

HELLO {FIRSTNAME} {LASTNAME},
THANK YOU FOR CREATING A CUSTOMER ACCOUNT AT {SHOP_NAME}.

YOUR {SHOP_NAME} LOGIN DETAILS

Here are your login details:
E-mail address: {email}
Password: {passwd}

IMPORTANT SECURITY TIPS:

1. Always keep your account details safe.
2. Never disclose your login details to anyone.
3. Change your password regularly.
4. Should you suspect someone is using your account illegally, please notify us immediately.

You can now book on: {shop_name}

{shop_name} is part of Havana Digital Enterprises™

Figure 3-32. *Editing e-mail template*

Every text enclosed in {text} represents variables that are supplied to e-mail templates. Consequently, {email}, {passwd}, and {shop_name} are all variables for the account e-mail template.

3-10. Adding New Variables to E-mail Templates

Problem

You want to add new variables to e-mail templates to display additional information.

Solution

In the first stage, we'll assume we want to add a new variable to the account e-mail template. Later, we'll focus on adding a new variable to the order confirmation e-mail template. To solve the first case, we'll edit the AuthController.php file so let's start by copying it to the override/controllers/front folder.

How It Works

In the AuthController.php file, at the end, locate the sendConfirmationMail() method. (Listing 3-22)

Listing 3-22. Method for Sending Confirmation E-mail after Customer Registration

```
protected function sendConfirmationMail(Customer $customer)
    {
        if (!Configuration::get('PS_CUSTOMER_CREATION_EMAIL')) {
            return true;
        }

        return Mail::Send(
            $this->context->language->id,
            'account',
            Mail::l('Welcome!'),
```

```
        array(
            '{firstname}' => $customer->firstname,
            '{lastname}' => $customer->lastname,
            '{email}' => $customer->email,
            '{passwd}' => Tools::getValue('passwd')),
        $customer->email,
        $customer->firstname.' '.$customer->lastname
    );
}
```

The Send() static method of the Mail class has the following signature:

```
public static function Send($id_lang, $template, $subject, $template_vars, $to,
$to_name = null, $from = null, $from_name = null, $file_attachment = null, $mode_smtp =
null,$template_path = _PS_MAIL_DIR_, $die = false, $id_shop = null, $bcc = null, $reply_to =
null)
```

The second argument indicates the template to be used; in this case, the "account" template. Only the first five arguments are mandatory; the fourth should be an array of variables to be included in the e-mail template. If we need to add the customer company field to the template, we just need to make the next modification to the method shown in Listing 3-22. (Listing 3-23)

Listing 3-23. Method for Sending Confirmation E-mail Adding Customer Company as New Variable

```
protected function sendConfirmationMail(Customer $customer)
    {
        if (!Configuration::get('PS_CUSTOMER_CREATION_EMAIL')) {
            return true;
        }

        return Mail::Send(
            $this->context->language->id,
            'account',
            Mail::l('Welcome!'),
            array(
'{company}' => $customer->company,
                '{firstname}' => $customer->firstname,
                '{lastname}' => $customer->lastname,
                '{email}' => $customer->email,
                '{passwd}' => Tools::getValue('passwd')),
            $customer->email,
            $customer->firstname.' '.$customer->lastname
        );
    }
```

The modification basically consists in adding the new company variable to the variables array.

Now we just need to go to PS Back Office, follow the path Localization->Translations, and edit the Account e-mail template to add the company variable to the template (Figure 3-33).

Figure 3-33. *Adding company variable to e-mail template*

Let's focus now on the second part of this recipe: adding a new variable to the order confirmation e-mail.

Order confirmation e-mails are usually issued by payment modules, and most payment modules derived from the PaymentModule class found in the file of the same name located in the classes folder in the PS package.

If we open PaymentModule.php, we'll find a method called validateOrder(), whose signature is the following:

```
public function validateOrder($id_cart, $id_order_state, $amount_paid, $payment_method =
'Unknown', $message = null, $extra_vars = array(), $currency_special = null, $dont_touch_
amount = false, $secure_key = false, Shop $shop = null)
```

The $extra_vars variable is an array where you can specify new variables that can be passed on to the "order" e-mail template. Since most payment modules inherit from the PaymentModule class, this method is available in all of them.

Another way to add new variables to the template would be to find the Mail::Send() function within the validateOrder() function and add the extra data as we did in the previous case, that is, submitting data in an array that is later specified as the four argument of the function.

3-11. Modifying the Social Networking Module to Add a TripAdvisor Link

Problem

You want to modify the Social Links module to add your TripAdvisor link or any other social account link to the footer.

Solution

If we look at the upper right corner of our PrestaShop's footer, we'll see a list of social links that bind our site to social profiles in various networks as shown in Figure 3-34.

Follow us

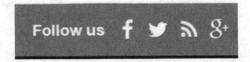

Figure 3-34. Social links

These links can be set in the PS Back Office by configuring the Social Networking module (Figure 3-35).

Front office Features
Social networking block v1.2.1 - by PrestaShop
Allows you to add information about your brand's social networking accounts.
Configure

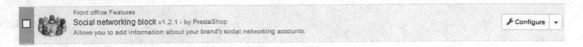

Figure 3-35. Social Networking module

The configuration page of this module is depicted in Figure 3-36.

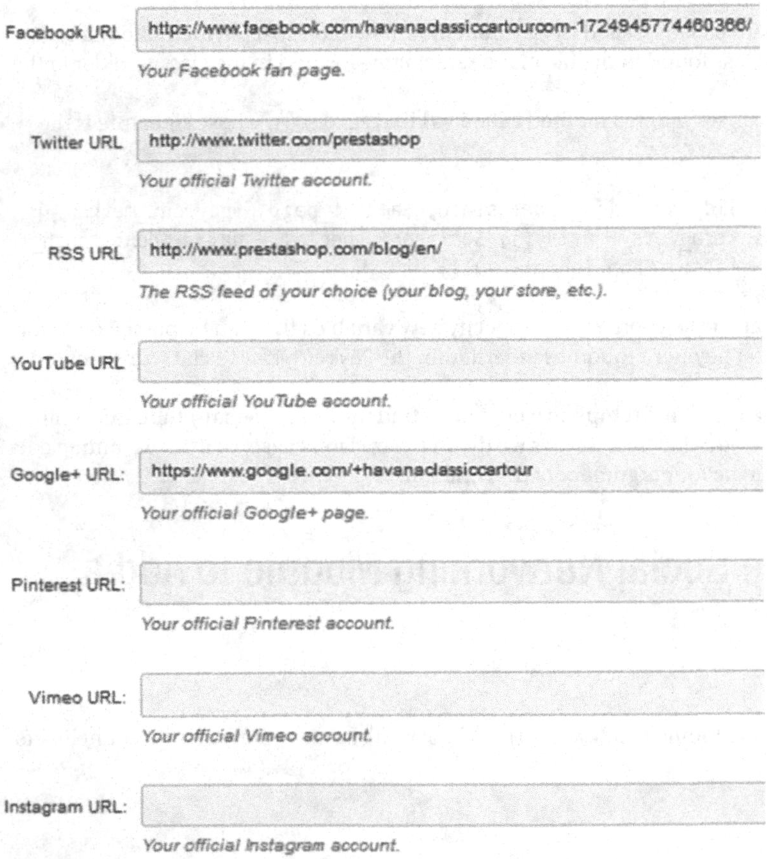
Facebook URL
https://www.facebook.com/havanaclassiccartourcom-1724945774460366/
Your Facebook fan page.
Twitter URL
http://www.twitter.com/prestashop
Your official Twitter account.
RSS URL
http://www.prestashop.com/blog/en/
The RSS feed of your choice (your blog, your store, etc.).
YouTube URL
Your official YouTube account.
Google+ URL:
https://www.google.com/+havanaclassiccartour
Your official Google+ page.
Pinterest URL:
Your official Pinterest account.
Vimeo URL:
Your official Vimeo account.
Instagram URL:
Your official Instagram account.

Figure 3-36. Configuration page of Social Networking module

As we can see, it allows us to define links for some of the most popular social networks. Notice some of the important ones are missing, TripAdvisor for example. Thus, in order to add the TripAdvisor URL or any other social network URL (this recipe can be easily generalized), we'll edit and customize the Social Networking module.

How It Works

The first thing we must do is guarantee our FontAwesome font package contains the TripAdvisor icon. The easiest way to achieve this is by downloading and replacing the current package with the latest. In this case, we used FontAwesome 4.7.0 and replaced every file in it with its corresponding match on themes/your_theme/fonts and themes/your_theme/css/font-awesome.

■ **Note** To update your FontAwesome font package, you need to replace every .eot, .svg, .ttf, .otf, .woff, and .woff2 files in your theme with files from the new package. You also need to replace the font-awesome.css file.

Now that we have everything in place, it's time to edit the Social Networking module. We'll start with the blocksocial.php file, so let's locate its install() method. (Listing 3-24)

Listing 3-24. Install() Method in blocksocial.php File

```
public function install()
    {
    return(parent::install()AND Configuration::updateValue('BLOCKSOCIAL_FACEBOOK', '') &&
                Configuration::updateValue('BLOCKSOCIAL_TWITTER', '') &&
                Configuration::updateValue('BLOCKSOCIAL_RSS', '') &&
                Configuration::updateValue('BLOCKSOCIAL_YOUTUBE', '') &&
                Configuration::updateValue('BLOCKSOCIAL_GOOGLE_PLUS', '')&&
                Configuration::updateValue('BLOCKSOCIAL_PINTEREST', '') &&
                Configuration::updateValue('BLOCKSOCIAL_VIMEO', '') &&
                Configuration::updateValue('BLOCKSOCIAL_INSTAGRAM', '') &&
                $this->registerHook('displayHeader') &&
                $this->registerHook('displayFooter'));
    }
```

Using the Configuration object, various configurations variables are saved into database. Thus, we'll need to add a TripAdvisor variable to consider this social network in future configuration and once we reinstall our module. Let's modify the previous code to contemplate a new BLOCKSOCIAL_TRIPADVISOR variable. (Listing 3-25)

Listing 3-25. Install() Method after Adding BLOCKSOCIAL_TRIPADVISOR Variable

```
public function install()
    {
    return (parent::install()AND
                Configuration::updateValue('BLOCKSOCIAL_FACEBOOK', '') &&
                Configuration::updateValue('BLOCKSOCIAL_TWITTER', '') &&
                Configuration::updateValue('BLOCKSOCIAL_RSS', '') &&
```

```
                        Configuration::updateValue('BLOCKSOCIAL_YOUTUBE', '') &&
                        Configuration::updateValue('BLOCKSOCIAL_GOOGLE_PLUS', '')&&
                        Configuration::updateValue('BLOCKSOCIAL_PINTEREST', '') &&
                        Configuration::updateValue('BLOCKSOCIAL_VIMEO', '') &&
                        Configuration::updateValue('BLOCKSOCIAL_INSTAGRAM', '') &&
                        Configuration::updateValue('BLOCKSOCIAL_TRIPADVISOR', '') &&
                            $this->registerHook('displayHeader') &&
                            $this->registerHook('displayFooter'));
        }
```

In the uninstall() method, we'll also need to add a line for deleting the BLOCKSOCIAL_TRIPADVISOR configuration variable. (Listing 3-26)

Listing 3-26. Uninstall() Method after Adding Line to Delete BLOCKSOCIAL_TRIPADVISOR Variable

```
public function uninstall()
        {
                //Delete configuration
                return (Configuration::deleteByName('BLOCKSOCIAL_FACEBOOK') AND
                        Configuration::deleteByName('BLOCKSOCIAL_TWITTER') AND
                        Configuration::deleteByName('BLOCKSOCIAL_RSS') AND
                        Configuration::deleteByName('BLOCKSOCIAL_YOUTUBE') AND
                        Configuration::deleteByName('BLOCKSOCIAL_GOOGLE_PLUS') AND
                        Configuration::deleteByName('BLOCKSOCIAL_PINTEREST') AND

                        Configuration::deleteByName('BLOCKSOCIAL_TRIPADVISOR') AND
                        Configuration::deleteByName('BLOCKSOCIAL_VIMEO') AND
                        Configuration::deleteByName('BLOCKSOCIAL_INSTAGRAM') AND
                        parent::uninstall());
        }
```

Next we need to modify the getContent() method. Remember this is the method responsible for updating any configuration variable shown on the PS Back Office, so this method will be triggered when we click the Configure button of any module. (Listing 3-27)

Listing 3-27. getContent() Method Modified

```
public function getContent()
        {
                // If we try to update the settings
                $output = '';
                if (Tools::isSubmit('submitModule'))
                {
                        Configuration::updateValue('BLOCKSOCIAL_FACEBOOK',
                        Tools::getValue('blocksocial_facebook', ''));
                        Configuration::updateValue('BLOCKSOCIAL_TWITTER',
                        Tools::getValue('blocksocial_twitter', ''));
                        Configuration::updateValue('BLOCKSOCIAL_RSS',
                        Tools::getValue('blocksocial_rss', ''));
                        Configuration::updateValue('BLOCKSOCIAL_YOUTUBE',
                        Tools::getValue('blocksocial_youtube', ''));
```

```
                    Configuration::updateValue('BLOCKSOCIAL_GOOGLE_PLUS',
                    Tools::getValue('blocksocial_google_plus', ''));
                    Configuration::updateValue('BLOCKSOCIAL_PINTEREST',
                    Tools::getValue('blocksocial_pinterest', ''));
                    Configuration::updateValue('BLOCKSOCIAL_VIMEO',
                    Tools::getValue('blocksocial_vimeo', ''));
                    Configuration::updateValue('BLOCKSOCIAL_INSTAGRAM',
                    Tools::getValue('blocksocial_instagram', ''));
                    Configuration::updateValue('BLOCKSOCIAL_TRIPADVISOR',
                    Tools::getValue('blocksocial_tripadvisor', ''));
                    $this->_clearCache('blocksocial.tpl');
                    Tools::redirectAdmin($this->context->link->getAdminLink
                    ('AdminModules').'&configure='.$this->name.'&tab_module='.$this->
                    tab.'&conf=4&module_name='.$this->name);
            }

            return $output.$this->renderForm();
        }
```

We must also modify the hookDisplayFooter() method to contemplate a new TripAdvisor link. This is the method responsible for rendering content when the displayFooter hook is executed on the footer and in your .tpl files. (Listing 3-28)

Listing 3-28. hookDisplayFooter() Method Modified

```
public function hookDisplayFooter()
        {
                if (!$this->isCached('blocksocial.tpl', $this->getCacheId()))
                        $this->smarty->assign(array(
                                'facebook_url' => Configuration::get('BLOCKSOCIAL_FACEBOOK'),
                                'twitter_url' => Configuration::get('BLOCKSOCIAL_TWITTER'),
                                'rss_url' => Configuration::get('BLOCKSOCIAL_RSS'),
                                'youtube_url' => Configuration::get('BLOCKSOCIAL_YOUTUBE'),
                                'google_plus_url' => Configuration::get('BLOCKSOCIAL_GOOGLE_
                                PLUS'),
                                'pinterest_url' => Configuration::get('BLOCKSOCIAL_
                                PINTEREST'),
                                'vimeo_url' => Configuration::get('BLOCKSOCIAL_VIMEO'),
                                'instagram_url' => Configuration::get('BLOCKSOCIAL_
                                INSTAGRAM'),
                                                        'tripadvisor_url' =>
                                                        Configuration::get('BLOCKSOCIAL_
                                                        TRIPADVISOR'),
                        ));

                return $this->display(__FILE__, 'blocksocial.tpl', $this->getCacheId());
        }
```

To show the textbox allowing us to define the URL for our TripAdvisor account, we need to add that field to the form presented on the module's configuration page; we can do this by editing the $fields_form variable of the renderForm() method as shown in Listing 3-29.

Listing 3-29. Adding TripAdvisor Field to $fields_form Variable in renderForm() Method

```
$fields_form = array(
                'form' => array(
                    'legend' => array(
                        'title' => $this->l('Settings'),
                        'icon' => 'icon-cogs'
                    ),
                    'input' => array(
                        array(
                            'type' => 'text',
                            'label' => $this->l('Facebook URL'),
                            'name' => 'blocksocial_facebook',
                            'desc' => $this->l('Your Facebook fan page.'),
                        ),
                        array(
                            'type' => 'text',
                            'label' => $this->l('Twitter URL'),
                            'name' => 'blocksocial_twitter',
                            'desc' => $this->l('Your official Twitter
                            account.'),
                        ),
                        array(
                            'type' => 'text',
                            'label' => $this->l('RSS URL'),
                            'name' => 'blocksocial_rss',
                            'desc' => $this->l('The RSS feed of your
                            choice (your blog, your store, etc.).'),
                        ),
                        array(
                            'type' => 'text',
                            'label' => $this->l('YouTube URL'),
                            'name' => 'blocksocial_youtube',
                            'desc' => $this->l('Your official YouTube
                            account.'),
                        ),
                        array(
                            'type' => 'text',
                            'label' => $this->l('Google+ URL:'),
                            'name' => 'blocksocial_google_plus',
                            'desc' => $this->l('Your official Google+
                            page.'),
                        ),
                        array(
                            'type' => 'text',
                            'label' => $this->l('Pinterest URL:'),
                            'name' => 'blocksocial_pinterest',
                            'desc' => $this->l('Your official Pinterest
                            account.'),
                        ),
```

```
                               array(
                                       'type' => 'text',
                                       'label' => $this->l('Vimeo URL:'),
                                       'name' => 'blocksocial_vimeo',
                                       'desc' => $this->l('Your official Vimeo
                                       account.'),
                               ),
                               array(
                                       'type' => 'text',
                                       'label' => $this->l('Instagram URL:'),
                                       'name' => 'blocksocial_instagram',
                                       'desc' => $this->l('Your official Instagram
                                       account.'),
                               ),
                               array(
                                       'type' => 'text',
                    'label' => $this->l('TripAdvisor URL:'),
                    'name' => 'blocksocial_tripadvisor',
            'desc' => $this->l('Your official Instagram account.'),

                                       ),
                               ),
                               'submit' => array(
                                       'title' => $this->l('Save'),
                               )
                       ),
               );
```

Finally, to be able to see in the Configuration page the values we previously set for each social link, we edit the getConfigFieldsValues() method adding the TripAdvisor reference. (Listing 3-30)

Listing 3-30. getConfigFieldsValues () Method Modified

```
public function getConfigFieldsValues()
        {
               return array(
                       'blocksocial_facebook' => Tools::getValue('blocksocial_facebook',
                       Configuration::get('BLOCKSOCIAL_FACEBOOK')),
                       'blocksocial_twitter' => Tools::getValue('blocksocial_twitter',
                       Configuration::get('BLOCKSOCIAL_TWITTER')),
                       'blocksocial_rss' => Tools::getValue('blocksocial_rss',
                       Configuration::get('BLOCKSOCIAL_RSS')),
                       'blocksocial_youtube' => Tools::getValue('blocksocial_youtube',
                       Configuration::get('BLOCKSOCIAL_YOUTUBE')),
                       'blocksocial_google_plus' => Tools::getValue('blocksocial_google_
                       plus', Configuration::get('BLOCKSOCIAL_GOOGLE_PLUS')),
                       'blocksocial_pinterest' => Tools::getValue('blocksocial_pinterest',
                       Configuration::get('BLOCKSOCIAL_PINTEREST')),
                       'blocksocial_vimeo' => Tools::getValue('blocksocial_vimeo',
                       Configuration::get('BLOCKSOCIAL_VIMEO')),
                       'blocksocial_instagram' => Tools::getValue('blocksocial_instagram',
                       Configuration::get('BLOCKSOCIAL_INSTAGRAM')),
```

111

```
                    'blocksocial_tripadvisor' => Tools::getValue('blocksocial_
                    tripadvisor', Configuration::get('BLOCKSOCIAL_TRIPADVISOR')),
            );
    }
```

Now that we have completely edited the blocksocial.php file, it's time to modify the front-end piece of the module. Go to themes/your_theme/modules/blocksocial and open the file blocksocial.tpl. (Listing 3-31).

Listing 3-31. blocksocial.tpl File of Your Theme Modified

```
<div id="social_block">
        <h4 class="title_block">{l s='Follow us' mod='blocksocial'}</h4>
        <ul>
                {if $facebook_url != ''}<li class="facebook"><a class="_blank"
                href="{$facebook_url|escape:html:'UTF-8'}">{l s='Facebook'
                mod='blocksocial'}</a></li>{/if}
                {if $twitter_url != ''}<li class="twitter"><a class="_blank"
                href="{$twitter_url|escape:html:'UTF-8'}">{l s='Twitter'
                mod='blocksocial'}</a></li>{/if}
                {if $rss_url != ''}<li class="rss"><a class="_blank" href="{$rss_
                url|escape:html:'UTF-8'}">{l s='RSS' mod='blocksocial'}</a></li>{/if}
                {if $youtube_url != ''}<li class="youtube"><a class="_blank"
                href="{$youtube_url|escape:html:'UTF-8'}">{l s='YouTube'
                mod='blocksocial'}</a></li>{/if}
                {if $google_plus_url != ''}<li class="google_plus"><a class="_blank"
                href="{$google_plus_url|escape:html:'UTF-8'}" rel="publisher">{l s='Google+'
                mod='blocksocial'}</a></li>{/if}
                {if $pinterest_url != ''}<li class="pinterest"><a class="_blank"
                href="{$pinterest_url|escape:html:'UTF-8'}">{l s='Pinterest'
                mod='blocksocial'}</a></li>{/if}
                {if $vimeo_url != ''}<li class="vimeo"><a href="{$vimeo_
                url|escape:html:'UTF-8'}">{l s='Vimeo' mod='blocksocial'}</a></li>{/if}
                {if $instagram_url != ''}<li class="instagram"><a class="_blank"
                href="{$instagram_url|escape:html:'UTF-8'}">{l s='Instagram'
                mod='blocksocial'}</a></li>{/if}
                {if $tripadvisor_url != ''}<li class="tripadvisor"><a class="_blank"
                href="{$tripadvisor_url|escape:html:'UTF-8'}">{l s='TripAdvisor'
                mod='blocksocial'}</a></li>{/if}
        </ul>
</div>
```

The modification to the Smarty template rendered on the displayFooter hook is very simple; we just add one final li HTML element in case the TripAdvisor URL has been set in the Back Office.

A final step is required to make our new TripAdvisor link work; we need to define a CSS rule that would load the TripAdvisor icon from our newly uploaded FontAwesome font package. For this purpose, we'll edit the global.css file found in themes/your_theme/css adding the rule in Listing 3-32.

Listing 3-32. CSS Rule to Show TripAdvisor Icon

```
.footer-container #footer #social_block ul li.tripadvisor a:before {
        content: "\f262"; }
```

Having everything edited, we can visit the PS Back Office, find the Social Networking module, and add our TripAdvisor link as seen in Figure 3-37.

Modules and Services / blocksocial / ⚙ Configure

Configure
Social networking block

Back Translate Check update Manage hooks

Twitter URL

Your official Twitter account.

RSS URL

The RSS feed of your choice (your blog, your store, etc.).

YouTube URL

Your official YouTube account.

Google+ URL: https://www.google.com/+havanaclassiccartour

Your official Google+ page.

Pinterest URL:

Your official Pinterest account.

Vimeo URL:

Your official Vimeo account.

Instagram URL:

Your official Instagram account.

TripAdvisor URL: https://www.tripadvisor.com/Attraction_Review-g147271-d11710306-Reviews-Havana_Classic_Car_Tour-Havana_Ciudad_de_la_Habana_Province_Cuba.html

Your official Instagram account.

Figure 3-37. *Defining the TripAdvisor link in the Configuration page of Social Networking module*

At last, we can now see the TripAdvisor link in our footer along with the rest of social links (Figure 3-38).

Figure 3-38. *TripAdvisor link in footer*

Even though we modified the Social Networking module to contemplate a TripAdvisor link, we could also have done the same with any other social network simply by changing the content attribute described in the CSS rule added to the `global.css` file.

■ **Note**   The content property is used to insert generated content with the `:before` and `:after` pseudo elements. In Listing 3-32, content contains the code for the TripAdvisor glyphicon. You can try to change the code and find some new icons.

3-12. Modifying the MyAccount Footer Module to Display Links of Interest List

Problem

You want to add a static list of Links of Interest for your business or website that will be displayed within the MyAccount module in the footer.

Solution

To solve this problem, we will edit the `blockmyaccountfooter.tpl` file in the `modules/blockmyaccountfooter/` directory as shown in Figure 3-39.

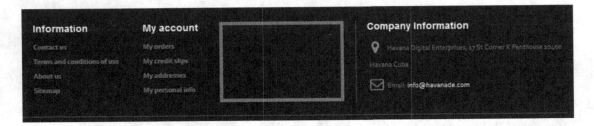

Figure 3-39. *Place to add the Links of Interests list*

The idea would be to place the list of links between the MyAccount module and the Contact Infos module as shown in figure 3-39.

How It Works

This is the content of the `blockmyaccountfooter.tpl` file located in `themes/your_theme/modules/blockmyaccountfooter`. (Listing 3-33)

Listing 3-33. Blockmyaccountfooter.tpl File in themes/your_theme/modules/blockmyaccountfooter

```
<section class="footer-block col-xs-12 col-sm-4">
        <h4><a href="{$link->getPageLink('my-account', true)|escape:'html':'UTF-8'}"
        title="{l s='Manage my customer account' mod='blockmyaccountfooter'}"
        rel="nofollow">{l s='My account' mod='blockmyaccountfooter'}</a></h4>
        <div class="block_content toggle-footer">
                <ul class="bullet">
```

```
        <li><a href="{$link->getPageLink('history', true)|escape:'html':'UTF-8'}"
        title="{l s='My orders' mod='blockmyaccountfooter'}" rel="nofollow">{l
        s='My orders' mod='blockmyaccountfooter'}</a></li>
        {if $returnAllowed}<li><a href="{$link->getPageLink('order-follow',
        true)|escape:'html':'UTF-8'}" title="{l s='My merchandise returns'
        mod='blockmyaccountfooter'}" rel="nofollow">{l s='My merchandise
        returns' mod='blockmyaccountfooter'}</a></li>{/if}
        <li><a href="{$link->getPageLink('order-slip',
        true)|escape:'html':'UTF-8'}" title="{l s='My credit slips'
        mod='blockmyaccountfooter'}" rel="nofollow">{l s='My credit slips'
        mod='blockmyaccountfooter'}</a></li>
        <li><a href="{$link->getPageLink('addresses',
        true)|escape:'html':'UTF-8'}" title="{l s='My addresses'
        mod='blockmyaccountfooter'}" rel="nofollow">{l s='My addresses'
        mod='blockmyaccountfooter'}</a></li>
        <li><a href="{$link->getPageLink('identity',
        true)|escape:'html':'UTF-8'}" title="{l s='Manage my personal
        information' mod='blockmyaccountfooter'}" rel="nofollow">{l s='My
        personal info' mod='blockmyaccountfooter'}</a></li>
        {if $voucherAllowed}<li><a href="{$link->getPageLink('discount',
        true)|escape:'html':'UTF-8'}" title="{l s='My vouchers'
        mod='blockmyaccountfooter'}" rel="nofollow">{l s='My vouchers'
        mod='blockmyaccountfooter'}</a></li>{/if}
        {$HOOK_BLOCK_MY_ACCOUNT}
    {if $is_logged}<li><a href="{$link->getPageLink('index')}?mylogout" title="{l
    s='Sign out' mod='blockmyaccountfooter'}" rel="nofollow">{l s='Sign out'
    mod='blockmyaccountfooter'}</a></li>{/if}
        </ul>
    </div>
</section>
```

We'll copy and paste the section HTML element and change the `col-sm-4` class to `col-sm-2` to split the space occupied by the MyAccount module in two equal parts. (Listing 3-34)

Listing 3-34. Blockmyaccountfooter.tpl File in themes/your_theme/modules/blockmyaccountfooter Modified

```
<!-- Block myaccount module -->
<section class="footer-block col-xs-12 col-sm-2">
    <h4><a href="{$link->getPageLink('my-account', true)|escape:'html':'UTF-8'}"
    title="{l s='Manage my customer account' mod='blockmyaccountfooter'}"
    rel="nofollow">{l s='My account' mod='blockmyaccountfooter'}</a></h4>
    <div class="block_content toggle-footer">
        <ul class="bullet">
            <li><a href="{$link->getPageLink('history',
            true)|escape:'html':'UTF-8'}" title="{l s='My orders'
            mod='blockmyaccountfooter'}" rel="nofollow">{l s='My orders'
            mod='blockmyaccountfooter'}</a></li>
            {if $returnAllowed}<li><a href="{$link->getPageLink('order-follow',
            true)|escape:'html':'UTF-8'}" title="{l s='My merchandise returns'
            mod='blockmyaccountfooter'}" rel="nofollow">{l s='My merchandise
            returns' mod='blockmyaccountfooter'}</a></li>{/if}
```

115

```
            <li><a href="{$link->getPageLink('order-slip',
            true)|escape:'html':'UTF-8'}" title="{l s='My credit slips'
            mod='blockmyaccountfooter'}" rel="nofollow">{l s='My credit slips'
            mod='blockmyaccountfooter'}</a></li>
            <li><a href="{$link->getPageLink('addresses',
            true)|escape:'html':'UTF-8'}" title="{l s='My addresses'
            mod='blockmyaccountfooter'}" rel="nofollow">{l s='My addresses'
            mod='blockmyaccountfooter'}</a></li>
            <li><a href="{$link->getPageLink('identity',
            true)|escape:'html':'UTF-8'}" title="{l s='Manage my personal
            information' mod='blockmyaccountfooter'}" rel="nofollow">{l s='My
            personal info' mod='blockmyaccountfooter'}</a></li>
            {if $voucherAllowed}<li><a href="{$link->getPageLink('discount',
            true)|escape:'html':'UTF-8'}" title="{l s='My vouchers'
            mod='blockmyaccountfooter'}" rel="nofollow">{l s='My vouchers'
            mod='blockmyaccountfooter'}</a></li>{/if}
            {$HOOK_BLOCK_MY_ACCOUNT}
        {if $is_logged}<li><a href="{$link->getPageLink('index')}?mylogout" title="{l
        s='Sign out' mod='blockmyaccountfooter'}" rel="nofollow">{l s='Sign out'
        mod='blockmyaccountfooter'}</a></li>{/if}
            </ul>
        </div>
</section>
<section class="footer-block col-xs-12 col-sm-2">
        <h4>Links of Interest</h4>
        <div class="block_content toggle-footer">
                <ul class="bullet">
                        <li><a href="http://www.internations.com">Internations</a></li>
                        <li><a href="http://www.tripadvisor.com">Trip Advisor</a></li>
                </ul>
        </div>
</section>
<!-- /Block myaccount module -->
```

We can now see the new links section next to the MyAccount list as illustrated in Figure 3-40.

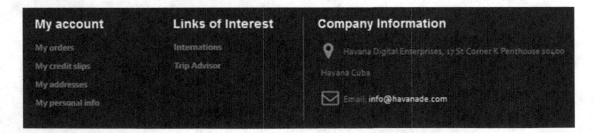

Figure 3-40. *Links of Interest list displayed in the footer*

In summary, the modification shown in this recipe consisted simply of changing the layout of the template by adding the new section and adjusting its size. In general, this is a very naïve approach for solving the problem at hand; a better, more elegant solution can be achieved if we create a module like we did in previous recipes that offers the possibility of setting the URL for each link of interest.

3-13. Generating Product Attributes by Adding Product Combinations

Problem

You want to define a set of attributes for your products.

Solution

Product attributes in PrestaShop are defined through combinations. To define attributes for one of your products, visit PS Back Office, go to Catalog->Products, and select one for editing; you'll see the Combinations tab on the left panel afterward.

How It Works

If we have an attribute A with values A1, A2, A3, and a second attribute B with values B1 and B2, then all combinations of these attributes would be A1-B1, A1-B2, A2-B1, A2-B2, A3-B1, and A3-B2. Generating all combinations by hand, especially when you have a large number of attributes, can be very difficult; for this reason, PS offers a tool known as Product Combination Generator (Figure 3-41).

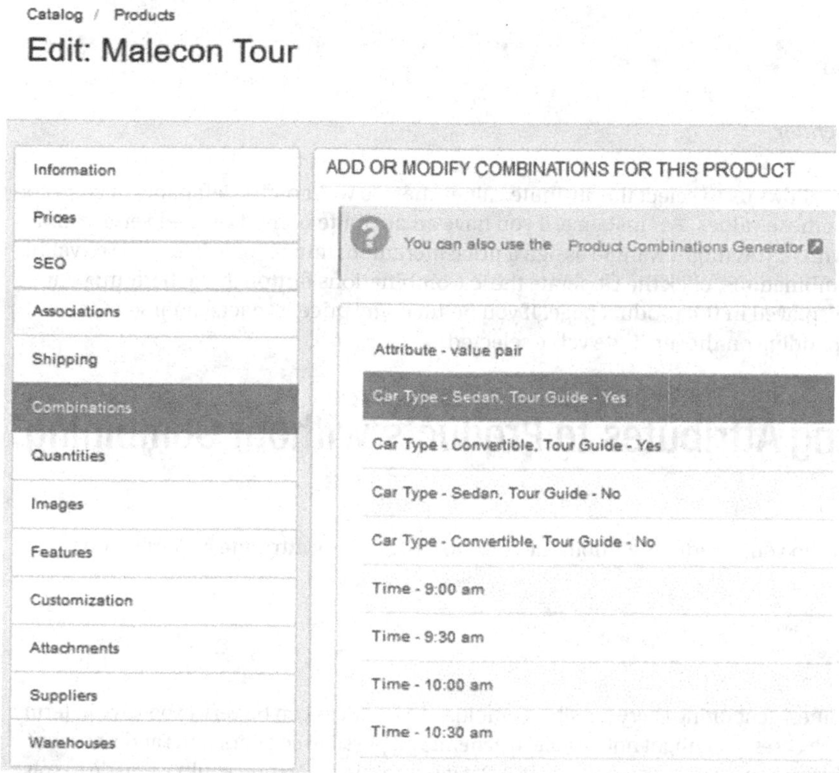

Catalog / Products

Edit: Malecon Tour

	ADD OR MODIFY COMBINATIONS FOR THIS PRODUCT
Information	
Prices	You can also use the Product Combinations Generator
SEO	
Associations	
Shipping	Attribute - value pair
Combinations	Car Type - Sedan, Tour Guide - Yes
Quantities	Car Type - Convertible, Tour Guide - Yes
Images	Car Type - Sedan, Tour Guide - No
Features	Car Type - Convertible, Tour Guide - No
Customization	Time - 9:00 am
Attachments	Time - 9:30 am
Suppliers	Time - 10:00 am
Warehouses	Time - 10:30 am

Figure 3-41. *Combinations section*

To use this tool, we first locate the Product Combinations Generator link on top of the Combinations tab and click it. This operation will take us to the Attributes generator seen in Figure 3-42.

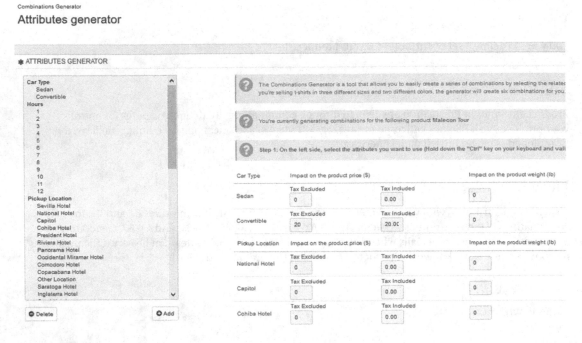

Figure 3-42. Attributes generator

The attribute generator allows us to select the attribute values that we want on the left panel to combine and assign price impacts on those values. For instance, if you have an attribute named Guided Service and values Yes, No associated with it, you might want to assign a price increment impact of $10 for the Yes value.

Finally, to generate combinations, click the Generate these Combinations button at the bottom; your product attributes will be displayed in the product page. If you defined any price impact, you'll see the product price changing depending on the attribute value selected.

3-14. Associating Attributes to Products without Combining

Problem

You want to assign attributes to your products without the need to assign every attribute as part of a combination.

Solution

When you have a lot of attributes, generating every possible combination for them can be very expensive in terms of computational time. In such cases, you might not be able to generate all possible combinations and a timeout or resource limits error might raise every time you try to do it. A PrestaShop customization could be made to solve this problem and create the possibility of associating only one attribute to a product. This customization will require us to edit the ajax-cart.js, `product.js` files located in the themes/your_theme/js folder.

How It Works

Let's assume we have a clothes-related product and we want to associate it to the Model attribute we'll shortly create, which has a lot of possible values.

We must first create the attribute and its values in the PS Back Office following path Catalog->Product Attributes and then clicking Add new attribute in the upper right corner (Figure 3-43).

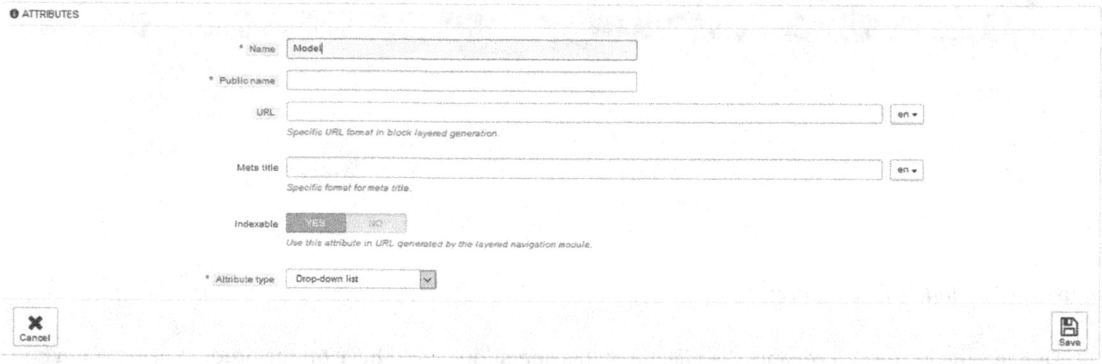

Figure 3-43. *Adding Model attribute*

The values we will add for this attribute will simply be A and B. Now, let us go to the Combinations tab of the clothes-related product and add the A value from the Model attribute. Click the New combination button in the lower right corner of the Combinations section and then select the Model attribute. In the dialog that shows up, select the A value, click Add, and to conclude the process click Save and Stay (Figure 3-44).

Figure 3-44. *Adding Model attribute as a combination of a single attribute*

We'll now be able to see the Model attribute listed in the combinations page as shown in Figure 3-45.

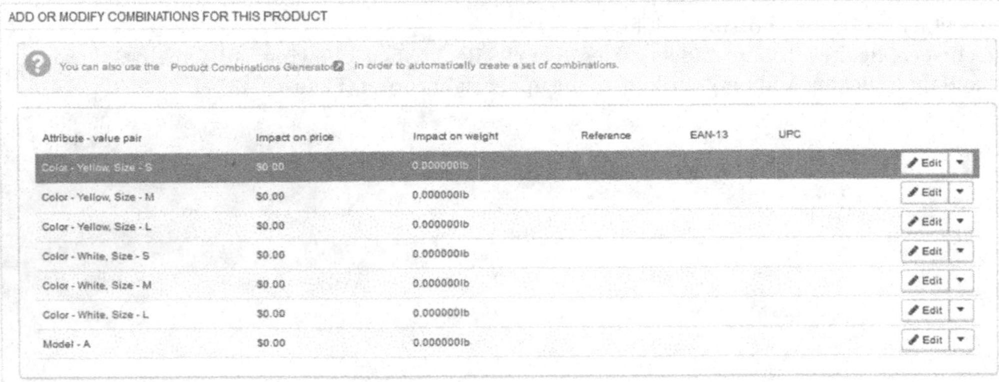

ADD OR MODIFY COMBINATIONS FOR THIS PRODUCT

You can also use the *Product Combinations Generator* in order to automatically create a set of combinations.

Attribute - value pair	Impact on price	Impact on weight	Reference	EAN-13	UPC	
Color - Yellow, Size - S	$0.00	0.000000lb				✎ Edit ▾
Color - Yellow, Size - M	$0.00	0.000000lb				✎ Edit ▾
Color - Yellow, Size - L	$0.00	0.000000lb				✎ Edit ▾
Color - White, Size - S	$0.00	0.000000lb				✎ Edit ▾
Color - White, Size - M	$0.00	0.000000lb				✎ Edit ▾
Color - White, Size - L	$0.00	0.000000lb				✎ Edit ▾
Model - A	$0.00	0.000000lb				✎ Edit ▾

Figure 3-45. *Model attribute added*

Depending on your PS version, the effect that this operation would have on the product page would be different. In older versions, the attribute will be apparently accepted, but after adding the product to cart the Cart Summary will not display the attribute's value, so in the end it will not be accepted. In recent versions, a message with the following text: "This combination does not exist for this product. Please select another combination." (Figure 3-46) will be displayed when you have a single attribute combination or when you have a combination that does not relate to the rest of attributes combinations.

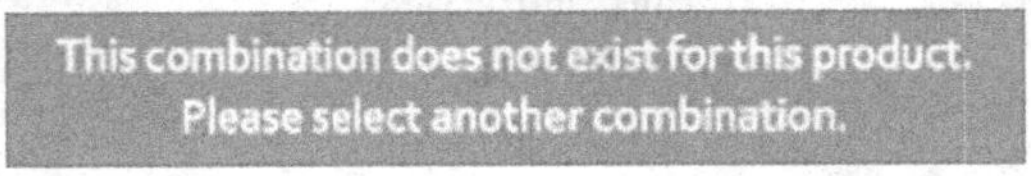

This combination does not exist for this product.
Please select another combination.

Figure 3-46. *Message displayed when product combination does not exist*

It's time to make the necessary modifications to our PS site, so any "independent" combination can be added to products and listed on the Cart Summary. We'll start by editing the themes/your_theme/js/product.js file.

To avoid getting the "This combination does not exist for this product. Please select another combination." Message, we'll edit the findCombinations() function located in the product.js file. (Listing 3-35)

Listing 3-35. First Lines of findCombinations() Method in product.js File

```
// search the combinations' case of attributes and update displaying of availability,
prices, ecotax, and image
function findCombination()
{
        $('#minimal_quantity_wanted_p').fadeOut();
        if (typeof $('#minimal_quantity_label').text() === 'undefined' || $('#minimal_
        quantity_label').html() > 1)
                $('#quantity_wanted').val(1);

        //create a temporary 'choice' array containing the choices of the customer
        var choice = [];
```

```
var radio_inputs = parseInt($('#attributes .checked > input[type=radio]').length);
if (radio_inputs)
        radio_inputs = '#attributes .checked > input[type=radio]';
else
        radio_inputs = '#attributes input[type=radio]:checked';

$('#attributes select, #attributes input[type=hidden], ' + radio_inputs).
each(function(){
        choice.push(parseInt($(this).val()));
});
```

The choice array in the previous code contains all attribute value selections made by the customer on the product page. We'll skip adding the value of our independent attributes. That way we won't receive any message and the Add to Cart button will be displayed. The modification is shown in Listing 3-36.

Listing 3-36. Modified Fragment of findCombinations() Method in product.js File

```
$('#attributes select, #attributes input[type=hidden], ' + radio_inputs).each(function(){
        if (!$(this).attr('model')) {
                choice.push(parseInt($(this).val()));
        }
});
```

Now, we will create a Custom field (also named Model) to contain the value selected for the Model attribute. When the customer clicks the Add to Cart button, the content of the Model attribute will be saved in the Model Custom field. Thus, it will be saved and listed in the Cart Summary, precisely our goal at this point.

Finally, we'll edit the themes/your_theme/js/modules/blockcart/ajax-cart.js file; near line 270 locate the code in Listing 3-37.

Listing 3-37. First Lines of Add Function in ajax-cart.js File

```
add : function(idProduct, idCombination, addedFromProductPage, callerElement, quantity,
whishlist){
                if (addedFromProductPage && !checkCustomizations())
                {
                        if (contentOnly)
                        {
                                var productUrl = window.document.location.href + '';
                                var data = productUrl.replace('content_only=1', '');
                                window.parent.document.location.href = data;
                                return;
                        }
                }
```

We'll assume you already read and implemented Recipe 3-5; it is a prerequisite for this recipe and part of its code.

The modification to the ajax-cart.js file is shown in Listing 3-38.

Listing 3-38. Modification to ajax-cart.js File

```
            // Getting value from model attribute in product box
            var model = $("#group_4 option:selected").text();
            // Getting value from model attribute in product box
$(".customization_block_input").val(model);

            // Code for saving custom fields
            // Product Box Custom Form
$('#quantityBackup').val($('#quantity_wanted').val());
                customAction = $('#customizationForm').attr('action');
                $('body select[id^="group_"]').each(function() {
                        customAction = customAction.replace(new RegExp(this.id +
                        '=\\d+'), this.id +'=' + this.value);
                });

            // ajax to product page with custom action
            var customization_entries = $('#customizationForm').serialize();

            $.ajax({
                        async:false,
                        type: 'POST',
                        data: customization_entries+ '&ajax=1',
                        dataType: 'json',
                        url: customAction
            })

            if (addedFromProductPage && !checkCustomizations())
            {
```

First, we get the model attribute value. That's the `$("#group_4 option:selected").text()` line. `#group_4` is the id that PS assigns to that field and it can be easily seen by inspecting the page (pressing Ctrl + Shift + I in Chrome or Q in Firefox). Second, we assign that value to the Model custom field; again, the `.customization_block_input` class can be seen using the page inspector most browsers today include. The rest of the code corresponds to saving custom fields.

After clicking the Add to Cart button, we will now see the `Model` attribute associated to the product in the Cart Summary (Figure 3-47).

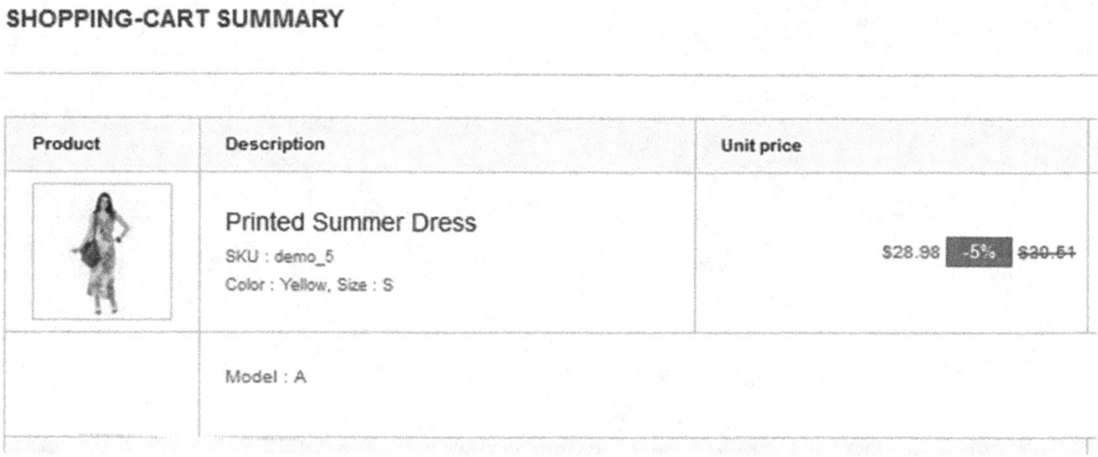

SHOPPING-CART SUMMARY

Product	Description	Unit price
	Printed Summer Dress SKU : demo_5 Color : Yellow, Size : S	$28.98 ~~-5%~~ ~~$30.51~~
	Model : A	

Figure 3-47. *Model attribute added to product and to Cart Summary*

For better esthetics, you can hide the entire customization form using the CSS Editing module;. In this manner, customers will not see the form on the product page and the entire process will seem cleaner for them.

Summary

In this chapter, we described various recipes that allow us to transform PS front end to many of our possible needs. We created a Testimonials module and we changed the layout of the page and the slider to make it more modern and sophisticated. We also customized the e-mail templates. In chapter 5, we will dive into the interesting topic of classes and controllers in PS.

CHAPTER 4

■ ■ ■

Classes and Controllers

The concept of class comes from the Object Oriented Programming (OOP) paradigm. In OOP the concepts of object and class are highly related. Objects are the main elements of this paradigm and they try to find correspondence with "real-life" objects. We could have an object named Dog that tries to represent a real-life dog incorporating many of its attributes (color, height, and so on) and its functionalities (bark, eat, sleep, and so on). To be able to create the Dog object, we would need a "blueprint" to follow or a "model" to build from; this blueprint or model is the class.

The class describes how the object will be in terms of attributes and functionalities. The object is the realization of such class. The object is tangible, whereas the class is more of a description of what the object is. PrestaShop was developed using PHP, an Object Oriented Programming language that incorporates the notions of class, objects, inheritance, and so on.

Inheritance is another concept associated with the OOP paradigm. It refers to the ability of one class to inherit from some other class, obtaining all of its methods and attributes. We'll check all of these concepts as we progress through the chapter in different recipes.

Controllers embody one of the main components of the MVC (Model-View-Controller) paradigm of which PrestaShop is a clear representative. In this paradigm, applications are commonly divided into three layers: the Model, related to database operations; the View, related to templates and everything we see on the browser (CSS, JS, and so on); and the Controller, related to the logic executed after the user requests a URL from your shop.

In this chapter, we'll examine various recipes for customizing your PrestaShop classes and controller. In many cases, these customizations will extend PS functionalities and behavior. You will learn the following:

- How to add a new field to the Product class

- How to add a new tab to the product edit page in PS Back Office

- How to add a new tab to the product edit page in Back Office using a module

- How to display a new product field on the product page

- How to enable combinations for virtual products

- How to send Order Confirmation messages to various recipients

- How to get a product price

- How to get product name and quantity

- How to get product categories and features

- How to get order total

© Arnaldo Pérez Castaño 2017
A. P. Castaño, *PrestaShop Recipes*, DOI 10.1007/978-1-4842-2574-5_4

■ **Note** PrestaShop classes can be found in the "classes" folder at the root of the PS package. Controllers can be found in the "controllers" folder also at the PS package root. Each controller file ends with the `Controller` suffix.

4-1. Adding a View Field to the Product Class

Problem

You want to add new fields to products of your PS site.

Solution

Let's assume we want to add a "booking dates" field to our PS products, perhaps to be able to know when a certain product/service has been booked or bought from our website. This field will be visible from the product edit page in the Back Office.

To achieve this customization, we'll change the `product` and `product_shop` tables in the PS database. We'll also change the `Product` class located in the `classes/Product.php` file and the `informations.tpl` template file located in `your_admin_folder/themes/default/template/controllers/products`.

■ **Note** Remember `your_admin_folder` is the "admin" folder that is originally in the PS package and is renamed when you install PS; it contains all files of the Back Office.

How It Works

To start, we'll copy the `classes/Product.php` file to the `override/classes` folder. Then we'll edit the `Product` class it contains by changing its name to "Product" and making it inherit from ProductCore. (Listing 4-1)

Listing 4-1. Renaming Class in override/classes/Product.php

```
class Product extends ProductCore {
    ...
}
```

Next, we'll add the `$booking_dates` variable, which will represent the new field of our PS products. We'll add it after the `$available_now` field variable, as shown in Listing 4-2.

Listing 4-2. Fragment of Product Class Where We Added the $booking_dates Variable

```
class ProductCore extends ObjectModel
{
    /** @var string Tax name */
    public $tax_name;

    /** @var string Tax rate */
    public $tax_rate;
```

```
    /** @var int Manufacturer id */
    public $id_manufacturer;

    /** @var int Supplier id */
    public $id_supplier;

    /** @var int default Category id */
    public $id_category_default;

    /** @var int default Shop id */
    public $id_shop_default;

    /** @var string Manufacturer name */
    public $manufacturer_name;

    /** @var string Supplier name */
    public $supplier_name;

    /** @var string Name */
    public $name;

    /** @var string Long description */
    public $description;

    /** @var string Short description */
    public $description_short;

    /** @var int Quantity available */
    public $quantity = 0;

    /** @var int Minimal quantity for add to cart */
    public $minimal_quantity = 1;

    /** @var string available_now */
    public $available_now;

/** @var string available_now */
public $booking_dates;

    /** @var string available_later */
    public $available_later;
```

To finalize the edits to the Product class, we need to add it to the $definition array defining its type (STRING) and the way it will be validated. (Listing 4-3)

Listing 4-3. Fragment of $definition Array in Product Class Where We Added the booking_dates Field

```
public static $definition = array(
        'table' => 'product',
        'primary' => 'id_product',
        'multilang' => true,
        'multilang_shop' => true,
```

```
'fields' => array(
    /* Classic fields */
    'id_shop_default' =>              array('type' => self::TYPE_INT, 'validate' =>
                                      'isUnsignedId'),
    'id_manufacturer' =>              array('type' => self::TYPE_INT, 'validate' =>
                                      'isUnsignedId'),
    'id_supplier' =>                  array('type' => self::TYPE_INT, 'validate' =>
                                      'isUnsignedId'),
        'booking_dates' =>array('type' => self::TYPE_STRING, 'shop' => true,
                          'validate' => 'isGenericName'),
...
```

After making these modifications to the Product class, it's time to reflect them also in the PS database. For that purpose, we'll access phpMyAdmin and add a new booking_dates column to the product and product_shop tables.

Once you have accessed phpMyAdmin, select your PS database. In the top menu, click the Structure tab. Add the new column after the available_now column and as a varchar of length 255, accepting the Null value (Figure 4-1).

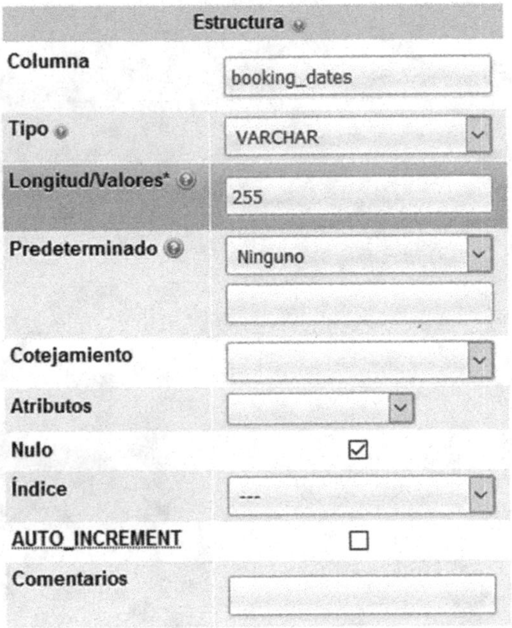

Figure 4-1. Defining new column booking_dates for product and product_shop tables

To conclude, we'll edit the your_admin_folder/themes/default/template/controllers/products/
informations.tpl file. This is the template file that displays the product edit page in the Back Office; let's
add a new div HTML element after the product-pack-container div. (Listing 4-4)

Listing 4-4. Fragment Added to informations.tpl template File

```
<div id="product-pack-container" {if $product_type != Product::PTYPE_PACK}
style="display:none"{/if}></div>
        <hr />
        {* Div element added *}
        <div class="form-group">
                <label class="control-label col-lg-3" for="youtube">
                        <span class="label-tooltip" data-toggle="tooltip"
                        title="{l s='Booking Dates'}">
                {l s='Booking Dates'}
                        </span>
                </label>
                <div class="col-lg-5">
                <input type="text" id="booking_dates" name="booking_dates" value="{$product-
                >booking_dates|htmlentitiesUTF8}"/>
                </div>
        </div>
```

Now we can go to the Back Office, edit a product, and see our new field available as depicted in Figure 4-2.

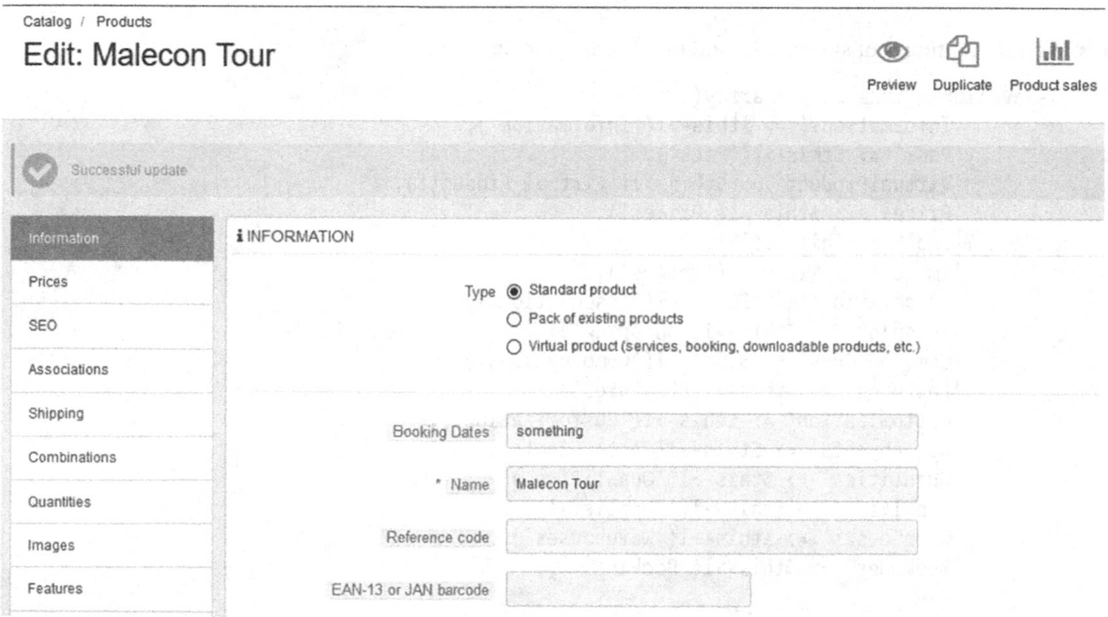

Figure 4-2. *Product page in PS Back Office with new booking dates field*

In this recipe, we showed how to create a new field to products in PS. In future recipes, we'll examine how to create new tabs for PS products.

4-2. Adding a New Tab to Product Edit Page in PS Back Office

Problem

You want to add a new tab to the product edit page in your PS Back Office, perhaps to show additional product fields or additional product information.

Solution

In this book, we'll present two solutions for adding a new tab to the product edit page in PS Back Office. The first one will be presented in this recipe and consist of directly modifying or overriding PrestaShop files to accomplish the desired customization; the second one consists of achieving the customization by developing and installing a module with the desired functionality (adding a new tab). This approach will be demonstrated in Recipe 4-3.

How It Works

In order to add a new tab, we'll need to edit the controllers/admin/AdminProductsController.php file. Once you have opened the file, locate the _construct() method, find the $this->available_tabs_lang and $this->available_tabs assignments, and add your new tab there as shown Listing 4-5.

Listing 4-5. Editing _construct() Method to Add New Bookings Tab

```
$this->available_tabs_lang = array(
        'Informations' => $this->l('Information'),
        'Pack' => $this->l('Pack'),
        'VirtualProduct' => $this->l('Virtual Product'),
        'Prices' => $this->l('Prices'),
        'Seo' => $this->l('SEO'),
        'Images' => $this->l('Images'),
        'Associations' => $this->l('Associations'),
        'Shipping' => $this->l('Shipping'),
        'Combinations' => $this->l('Combinations'),
        'Features' => $this->l('Features'),
        'Customization' => $this->l('Customization'),
        'Attachments' => $this->l('Attachments'),
        'Quantities' => $this->l('Quantities'),
        'Suppliers' => $this->l('Suppliers'),
        'Warehouses' => $this->l('Warehouses'),
        'Bookings' => $this->l('Bookings'),
    );
```

```
$this->available_tabs = array('Quantities' => 6, 'Warehouses' => 14);
if ($this->context->shop->getContext() != Shop::CONTEXT_GROUP) {
    $this->available_tabs = array_merge($this->available_tabs, array(
        'Informations' => 0,
        'Pack' => 7,
        'VirtualProduct' => 8,
        'Prices' => 1,
        'Seo' => 2,
        'Associations' => 3,
        'Images' => 9,
        'Shipping' => 4,
        'Combinations' => 5,
        'Features' => 10,
        'Customization' => 11,
        'Attachments' => 12,
        'Suppliers' => 13,
        'Bookings' => 15
    ));
}
```

For this example and following the approach introduced in Recipe 4-1, we'll create a bookings-related tab and we'll make use of the booking field added to products in Recipe 4-1.

The first array shown in Listing 4-5 allows us to indicate a translation string for every tab, and in the second one we define the name of each tab.

■ **Note**　In the available_tabs array, we define each tab name associated with a value that indicates its position in the left panel containing every tab. Consequently, changing or exchanging these numbers will change the order in which tabs are displayed on the product page.

Once we execute these simple edits, the new Bookings tab should be visible in the Back Office as illustrated in Figure 4-3.

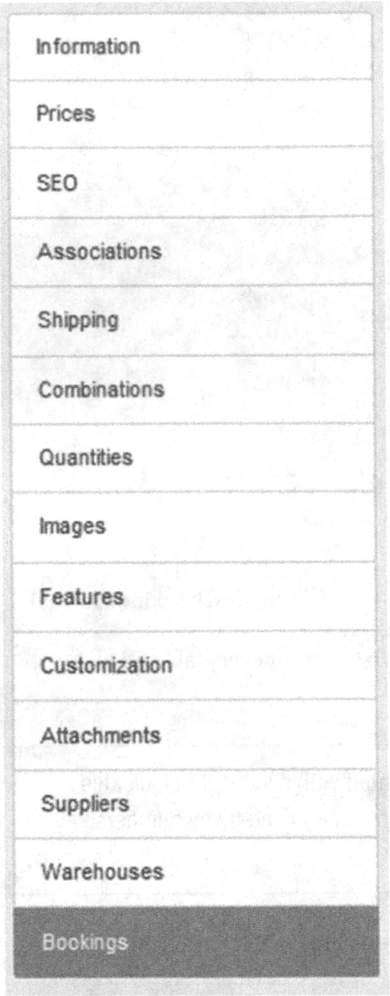

Information
Prices
SEO
Associations
Shipping
Combinations
Quantities
Images
Features
Customization
Attachments
Suppliers
Warehouses
Bookings

Figure 4-3. *Bookings tab in product editing page in PS Back Office*

If we click the tab now, we'll notice it is empty; it displays no content. How do we make it display a form showing a Booking Dates text field like the one we added in Recipe 4-1?

To display something on the tab, we need to create a `.tpl` file named exactly as the tab, in lowercase letters, and have it located at `your_admin_folder/themes/default/template/controllers/products`. In this case, the file would be `your_admin_folder/themes/default/template/controllers/products/bookings.tpl` (Figure 4-4).

combination

helpers

multishop

associations.tpl

attachments.tpl

bookings.tpl

combinations.tpl

customization.tpl

features.tpl

images.tpl

index.php

informations.tpl

input_text_lang.tpl

pack.tpl

Figure 4-4. *your_admin_folder/themes/default/template/controllers/products folder showing the bookings. tpl template file*

This is the content added to the bookings.tpl file. Part of it was obtained from the informations.tpl template. (Listing 4-6)

Listing 4-6. Content of bookings.tpl File

```
<div id="product-bookings" class="panel product-tab">
        <input type="hidden" name="submitted_tabs[]" value="Bookings" />
        <h3 class="tab"><i class="icon-info"></i> {l s='Booking'}</h3>

        <div class="form-group">
                <label class="control-label col-lg-3" for="booking_dates">
                        <span class="label-tooltip" data-toggle="tooltip"
                          title="{l s='Booking Dates'}">
                    {l s='Booking Dates'}
                        </span>
                </label>
                <div class="col-lg-5">
                <input type="text" id="booking_dates" name="booking_dates" value="{$product-
                >booking_dates|htmlentitiesUTF8}"/>
                </div>
        </div>
</div>
```

```
        <div class="panel-footer">
                <a href="{$link->getAdminLink('AdminProducts')|escape:'html':'UTF-8'}
                {if isset($smarty.request.page) && $smarty.request.page > 1}&amp;submitFil
                terproduct={$smarty.request.page|intval}{/if}" class="btn btn-default"><i
                class="process-icon-cancel"></i> {l s='Cancel'}</a>
                <button type="submit" name="submitAddproduct" class="btn btn-default
                pull-right" disabled="disabled"><i class="process-icon-loading"></i>
                {l s='Save'}</button>
                <button type="submit" name="submitAddproductAndStay" class="btn btn-default
                pull-right" disabled="disabled"><i class="process-icon-loading"></i>
                {l s='Save and stay'}</button>
        </div>
</div>
```

The "form-group" div element code is the same we used in Recipe 4-1. The "panel-footer" div element defines the lower part division found in most sections of the Back Office where you have the Save and Save and Stay buttons, or both as it's in the product edit page.

Now we can see some content in the Bookings tab as shown in Figure 4-5.

Figure 4-5. Bookings section on product edit page

In the next section, we'll see how to accomplish the same result by using a module instead of overriding or directly editing PS files.

4-3. Adding a New Tab to the Product Edit Page in Back Office Using a Module

Problem

You want to add a new tab to the product edit page in your PS Back Office, perhaps to show additional product fields or additional product information, and you want that addition to occur through a module.

Solution

In order to solve this problem, we'll start by building the essential pieces of a module (.php and .tpl files) like we already know how to do from previous chapters. As we did in Recipe 4-2, we'll demonstrate how to add a new tab to the product edit page, creating a module related to bookings.

First, we create a bookings folder in the modules folder and then we add the files that we need for the moment; those are bookings.php and logo.png or logo.gif. The initial lines of the PHP main file (bookings.php) should look like Listing 4-7.

Listing 4-7. __construct() Method of Bookings Module

```php
<?php
if(!defined('_PS_VERSION_'))
        exit;

class Bookings extends Module {

        public function __construct()
    {
                $this->name = 'bookings';
                $this->tab = 'front_office_features';
                $this->version = '1.0.0';
                $this->author = 'Arnaldo Perez Castano';
                $this->need_instance = 0;
                $this->ps_versions_compliancy = array('min' => '1.6', 'max' => _PS_
                VERSION_);
                $this->bootstrap = true;

                parent::__construct();

                $this->displayName = $this->l('Bookings');
                $this->description = $this->l('Add Bookings Tab to product edit page');

                $this->confirmUninstall = $this->l('Are you sure you want to uninstall?');
        }
```

That should be enough to get our new module displayed in PS Back Office under the Modules and Services section, as illustrated in Figure 4-6.

Figure 4-6. *Bookings module displayed on module list in PS Back Office*

Let's take a look at the install() and uninstall() methods for this module in Listing 4-8.

Listing 4-8. Install() and uninstall() Methods for Bookings Module

```
public function install()
{
        if (!parent::install() ||
                !$this->registerHook('displayAdminProductsExtra'))
                return false;
        return true;
}

public function uninstall()
{
        if (!parent::uninstall())
                return false;
        return true;
}
```

Notice we are registering two hooks that we haven't studied yet. The displayAdminProductsExtra hook will allow us to add new tabs to product edit page, as shown in Listing 4-9.

Listing 4-9. hookdisplayAdminProductsExtra() Method

```
public function hookdisplayAdminProductsExtra($params)
    {
            $product = new Product((int)Tools::getValue('id_product'));
            if (Validate::isLoadedObject($product))
            {
                $this->context->smarty->assign(array(
                  'bookings' => $product->booking_dates
                                    ));

                    return $this->display(__FILE__, 'bookings.tpl');
            }
    }
```

In the displayAdminProductsExtra() method, we use the isLoadedObject() method of the Validate class to check whether the object has been correctly loaded. If it has, we assign the "bookings" Smarty variable and display the bookings.tpl template as seen in Figure 4-7.

Figure 4-7. *Result after installing the module*

As we can see in Figure 4-7, the result obtained is exactly the same achieved in Recipe 4-2. Also notice that in this recipe, as in Recipe 4-2, we assumed that the bookings_date field had already been added to the Product class and PS database.

■ **Note**   A hook that you may find useful when creating a new tab through a module is the actionProductUpdate hook, which is called when the product is changed and allows us to fetch data from our tab and process it.

4-4. Displaying a New Product Field on the Product Page

Problem

You have already created a new product column in the PS database and the corresponding new field in the Product class. Now you want to display that new field in the product page.

Solution

Maintaining the line we have been following throughout this chapter, let's assume we have a booking_dates field created on the PS database, specifically in the products table and the corresponding field in the Product class.

To display this new field on the product page, we just need to edit the product.tpl template file. In case we need to add some extra information or maybe make the code on the template file more legible, we could also edit the ProductController.php file.

How It Works

Recalling the new product field created in Recipe 4-1 and in case we are looking to add the new field to product page in its purest form, we simply need to add the code in Listing 4-10 (not considering HTML elements) in the place we feel appropriate in themes/your_theme/product.tpl.

Listing 4-10. Booking_dates Product Field Added to product.tpl

```
<h3> Booking {$product->booking_dates}</h3>
```

As we can see in Figure 4-8, the booking_dates field value will be now visible on the product page.

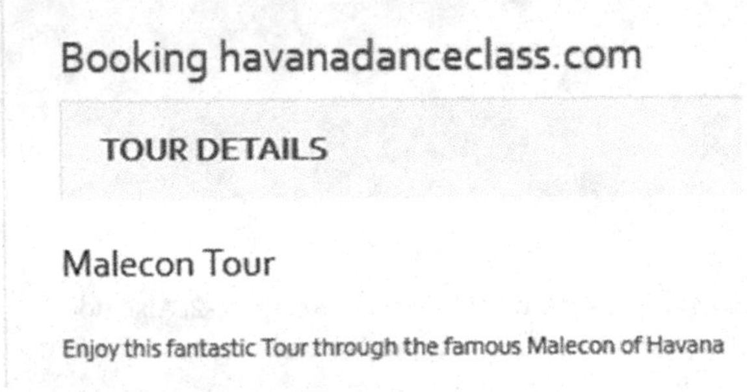

Booking havanadanceclass.com

TOUR DETAILS

Malecon Tour

Enjoy this fantastic Tour through the famous Malecon of Havana

Figure 4-8. *Value of booking_dates field displayed on product page*

If we would like to do something more complex than just the booking_dates field, maybe a pre-processing stage, we could add a new Smarty variable in the controllers/front/ProductController.php file that would encapsulate the result of this pre-processing stage.

Edit or override the ProductController.php file and locate the initContent() method. Almost at the end, you will see the code in Listing 4-11.

Listing 4-11. Smarty Variables Being Assigned in initContent() Method of ProductController Class

```
$this->context->smarty->assign(array(
            'stock_management' => Configuration::get('PS_STOCK_MANAGEMENT'),
            'customizationFields' => $customization_fields,
            'id_customization' => empty($customization_datas) ? null : $customization_
                            datas[0]['id_customization'],
            'accessories' => $accessories,
            'return_link' => $return_link,
            'product' => $this->product,
                        'booking' => $this->product->booking_dates,
            'product_manufacturer' => new Manufacturer((int)$this->product->id_
                            manufacturer, $this->context->language->id),
            'token' => Tools::getToken(false),
            'features' => $this->product->getFrontFeatures($this->context->language->id),
            'attachments' => (($this->product->cache_has_attachments) ? $this->product
                        ->getAttachments($this->context->language->id) : array()),
            'allow_oosp' => $this->product->isAvailableWhenOutOfStock((int)$this-
                        >product->out_of_stock),
            'last_qties' =>  (int)Configuration::get('PS_LAST_QTIES'),
```

```
'HOOK_EXTRA_LEFT' => Hook::exec('displayLeftColumnProduct'),
'HOOK_EXTRA_RIGHT' => Hook::exec('displayRightColumnProduct'),
'HOOK_PRODUCT_OOS' => Hook::exec('actionProductOutOfStock', array('product'
                        => $this->product)),
'HOOK_PRODUCT_ACTIONS' => Hook::exec('displayProductButtons',
                            array('product' => $this->product)),
'HOOK_PRODUCT_TAB' => Hook::exec('displayProductTab', array('product' =>
                        $this->product)),
'HOOK_PRODUCT_TAB_CONTENT' => Hook::exec('displayProductTabContent',
                                array('product' => $this->product)),
'HOOK_PRODUCT_CONTENT' => Hook::exec('displayProductContent',
                            array('product' => $this->product)),
'display_qties' => (int)Configuration::get('PS_DISPLAY_QTIES'),
'display_ht' => !Tax::excludeTaxeOption(),
'jqZoomEnabled' => Configuration::get('PS_DISPLAY_JQZOOM'),
'ENT_NOQUOTES' => ENT_NOQUOTES,
'outOfStockAllowed' => (int)Configuration::get('PS_ORDER_OUT_OF_STOCK'),
'errors' => $this->errors,
'body_classes' => array(
    $this->php_self.'-'.$this->product->id,
    $this->php_self.'-'.$this->product->link_rewrite,
    'category-'.(isset($this->category) ? $this->category->id : ''),
    'category-'.(isset($this->category) ? $this->category->getFieldByLang
    ('link_rewrite') : '')
),
'display_discount_price' => Configuration::get('PS_DISPLAY_DISCOUNT_PRICE'),
));
```

Insert in the previous array the name for your Smarty variable, followed by its content. it could be something like Listing 4-12.

Listing 4-12. Booking Smarty Variable

```
'booking' => 'Booking Dates are: '.$this->product->booking_dates
```

Then in the product.tpl file, you would just need to add the code in Listing 4-13.

Listing 4-13. Booking Smarty Variable Added to h3 Tag in product.tpl

```
<h3> {$booking}</h3>
```

As we can see, the result of the last code will be the text 'Booking Dates are: havanadanceclass.com'.

■ **Note**   Up to this moment, we have associated common strings as values for the booking_dates field. We could force to save only date strings by implementing some validation before the field is saved in the Back Office and the front end.

4-5. Enabling Combinations for Virtual Products

Problem

You want to enable the Combinations tab for virtual products.

Solution

In order to solve this problem, we'll need to edit the files `controllers/admin/AdminProductsController.php` and `your_admin_folder/themes/default/template/controllers/products/combinations.tpl` and `js/admin/products.js`.

How It Works

First, let's edit the `controllers/admin/AdminProductsController.php` file and locate the `initFormAttributes()` method, as seen in Listing 4-14.

Listing 4-14. First Lines of initFormAttributes() Method

```php
public function initFormAttributes($product)
    {
        $data = $this->createTemplate($this->tpl_form);
        if (!Combination::isFeatureActive()) {
            $this->displayWarning($this->l('This feature has been disabled. ').
                '<a href="index.php?tab=AdminPerformance&token='.Tools::getAdminTokenLite('A
                dminPerformance').'#featuresDetachables">'.$this->l('Performances').'</a>');
        } elseif (Validate::isLoadedObject($product)) {
            if ($this->product_exists_in_shop) {
                if ($product->is_virtual) {
                    $data->assign('product', $product);
                    $this->displayWarning($this->l('A virtual product cannot have
                    combinations.'));
                } else {
                    $attribute_js = array();
                    $attributes = Attribute::getAttributes($this->context->language->id, true);
                    foreach ($attributes as $k => $attribute) {
                        $attribute_js[$attribute['id_attribute_group']][$attribute
                        ['id_attribute']] = $attribute['name'];
                        natsort($attribute_js[$attribute['id_attribute_group']]);
                    }

                    $currency = $this->context->currency;

$data->assign('attributeJs', $attribute_js);
$data->assign('attributes_groups', AttributeGroup::getAttributesGroups($this->context-
>language->id));

                    $data->assign('currency', $currency);
```

```php
$images = Image::getImages($this->context->language->id, $product->id);

$data->assign('tax_exclude_option', Tax::excludeTaxeOption());
$data->assign('ps_weight_unit', Configuration::get('PS_WEIGHT_UNIT'));

$data->assign('ps_use_ecotax', Configuration::get('PS_USE_ECOTAX'));
$data->assign('field_value_unity', $this->getFieldValue
($product, 'unity'));

$data->assign('reasons', $reasons = StockMvtReason::getStockMvtReasons($
this->context->language->id));
$data->assign('ps_stock_mvt_reason_default', $ps_stock_mvt_reason_
default = Configuration::get('PS_STOCK_MVT_REASON_DEFAULT'));
$data->assign('minimal_quantity', $this->getFieldValue($product, 'minimal_
quantity') ? $this->getFieldValue($product, 'minimal_quantity') : 1);
$data->assign('available_date', ($this->getFieldValue($product,
'available_date') != 0) ? stripslashes(htmlentities($this-
>getFieldValue($product, 'available_date'), $this->context->
language->id)) : '0000-00-00');

$i = 0;
$type = ImageType::getByNameNType('%', 'products', 'height');
if (isset($type['name'])) {
    $data->assign('imageType', $type['name']);
} else {
    $data->assign('imageType', ImageType::getFormatedName('small'));
}
$data->assign('imageWidth', (isset($image_type['width']) ? (int)
($image_type['width']) : 64) + 25);
foreach ($images as $k => $image) {
    $images[$k]['obj'] = new Image($image['id_image']);
    ++$i;
}
$data->assign('images', $images);

$data->assign($this->tpl_form_vars);
$data->assign(array(
    'list' => $this->renderListAttributes($product, $currency),
    'product' => $product,
    'id_category' => $product->getDefaultCategory(),
    'token_generator' => Tools::getAdminTokenLite
    ('AdminAttributeGenerator'),
    'combination_exists' => (Shop::isFeatureActive() &&
    (Shop::getContextShopGroup()->share_stock) && count
    (AttributeGroup::getAttributesGroups($this->context->language->id))
    > 0 && $product->hasAttributes())
));
    }
}
```

Now let's get rid of the following if statement, as shown in Listing 4-15.

Listing 4-15. If Statement to Get Rid Of

```
if ($product->is_virtual) {
body-if
}
else {
body-else
}
```

Body-if and body-else represent the code within the if and else statements respectively. We maintain the bodies and eliminate the rest of the code so instead of having the lines shown in Listing 4-15, we would end up with the code in Listing 4-16.

Listing 4-16. Maintaining Bodies of if and else Statements

```
body-if
body-else
```

The final code would look like Listing 4-17.

Listing 4-17. initFormAttributes() Method Already Modified

```
public function initFormAttributes($product)
    {
        $data = $this->createTemplate($this->tpl_form);
        if (!Combination::isFeatureActive()) {
            $this->displayWarning($this->l('This feature has been disabled. ').
                ' <a href="index.php?tab=AdminPerformance&token='.Tools::getAdminTokenLite('A
                dminPerformance').'#featuresDetachables">'.$this->l('Performances').'</a>');
        } elseif (Validate::isLoadedObject($product)) {
            if ($this->product_exists_in_shop) {
                    $attribute_js = array();
                  $attributes = Attribute::getAttributes($this->context->language->id, true);
                    foreach ($attributes as $k => $attribute) {
                        $attribute_js[$attribute['id_attribute_group']][$attribute
                        ['id_attribute']] = $attribute['name'];
natsort($attribute_js[$attribute['id_attribute_group']]);
}

                $currency = $this->context->currency;

$data->assign('attributeJs', $attribute_js);
$data->assign('attributes_groups', AttributeGroup::getAttributesGroups
($this->context->language->id));

                $data->assign('currency', $currency);
```

```
$images = Image::getImages($this->context->language->id, $product->id);

$data->assign('tax_exclude_option', Tax::excludeTaxeOption());
$data->assign('ps_weight_unit', Configuration::get('PS_WEIGHT_UNIT'));

$data->assign('ps_use_ecotax', Configuration::get('PS_USE_ECOTAX'));
$data->assign('field_value_unity', $this->getFieldValue($product, 'unity'));

$data->assign('reasons', $reasons = StockMvtReason::getStockMvtReasons
($this->context->language->id));
$data->assign('ps_stock_mvt_reason_default', $ps_stock_mvt_reason_
default = Configuration::get('PS_STOCK_MVT_REASON_DEFAULT'));
$data->assign('minimal_quantity', $this->getFieldValue($product, 'minimal_
quantity') ? $this->getFieldValue($product, 'minimal_quantity') : 1);
$data->assign('available_date', ($this->getFieldValue($product,
'available_date') != 0) ? stripslashes(htmlentities
($this->getFieldValue($product, 'available_date'), $this->
context->language->id)) : '0000-00-00');

$i = 0;
$type = ImageType::getByNameNType('%', 'products', 'height');
if (isset($type['name'])) {
    $data->assign('imageType', $type['name']);
} else {
    $data->assign('imageType', ImageType::getFormatedName('small'));
}
$data->assign('imageWidth', (isset($image_type['width']) ? (int)
($image_type['width']) : 64) + 25);
foreach ($images as $k => $image) {
    $images[$k]['obj'] = new Image($image['id_image']);
    ++$i;
}
$data->assign('images', $images);

$data->assign($this->tpl_form_vars);
$data->assign(array(
    'list' => $this->renderListAttributes($product, $currency),
    'product' => $product,
    'id_category' => $product->getDefaultCategory(),
    'token_generator' => Tools::getAdminTokenLite('AdminAttribute
    Generator'),
    'combination_exists' => (Shop::isFeatureActive() &&
    (Shop::getContextShopGroup()->share_stock) && count(Attribute
    Group::getAttributesGroups($this->context->language->id)) > 0 &&
    $product->hasAttributes())
));

}
```

Next, we'll edit the your_admin_folder/themes/default/template/controllers/products/ combinations.tpl file. The first code line of this file is shown in Listing 4-18.

Listing 4-18. First Line of Code from combinations.tpl File

```
{if isset($product->id) && !$product->is_virtual}
```

We'll remove the !product->is_virtual condition to guarantee that combinations will be visible for virtual products.

Finally, we'll edit the js/admin/products.js file; this is the file responsible for hiding the Combinations tab when you click Virtual Product in the Informations tab. In this file, locate the function/ piece of code shown in Listing 4-19. It should be around line number 1080.

Listing 4-19. switchProductType Function in products.js

```
this.switchProductType = function(){
            if (product_type == product_type_pack)
            {
                    $('#pack_product').attr('checked', true);
            }
            else if (product_type == product_type_virtual)
            {
                    $('#virtual_product').attr('checked', true);
                    $('#condition').attr('disabled', true);
                    $('#condition option[value=new]').attr('selected', true);
            }
            else
            {
                    $('#simple_product').attr('checked', true);
            }

            $('input[name="type_product"]').on('click', function(e)
            {
                    // Reset settings
                    $('a[id*="VirtualProduct"]').hide();

                    $('#product-pack-container').hide();

                    $('div.is_virtual_good').hide();
                    $('#is_virtual').val(0);
                    tabs_manager.onLoad('VirtualProduct', function(){
                            $('#is_virtual_good').removeAttr('checked');
                    });

                    product_type = $(this).val();
                    $('#warn_virtual_combinations').hide();
                    $('#warn_pack_combinations').hide();
                    // until a product is added in the pack
                    // if product is PTYPE_PACK, save buttons will be disabled
                    if (product_type == product_type_pack)
                    {
                            if (has_combinations)
```

```
        {
                $('#simple_product').attr('checked', true);
                $('#warn_pack_combinations').show();
        }
        else
        {
                $('#product-pack-container').show();
                // If the pack tab has not finished loaded the
                changes will be made when the loading event is
                triggered
                $("#product-tab-content-Pack").bind('loaded',
                function(){
                        $('#ppack').val(1).attr('checked', true).
                        attr('disabled', true);
                });
                $("#product-tab-content-Quantities").bind('loaded',
                function(){
                        $('.stockForVirtualProduct').show();
                });

                $('a[id*="Combinations"]').hide();
                $('a[id*="Shipping"]').show();

                $('#condition').removeAttr('disabled');
            $('#condition option[value=new]').removeAttr('selected');
                $('.stockForVirtualProduct').show();
                // if pack is enabled, if you choose pack,
                automatically switch to pack page
        }
    }
// Else If to be modified -->
    else if (product_type == product_type_virtual)
    {
            if (has_combinations)
            {
                    $('#simple_product').attr('checked', true);
                    $('#warn_virtual_combinations').show();
            }
            else
            {
                    $('a[id*="VirtualProduct"]').show();
                    $('#is_virtual').val(1);

                    tabs_manager.onLoad('VirtualProduct', function(){
                        $('#is_virtual_good').attr('checked', true);
                        $('#virtual_good').show();
                    });

                    tabs_manager.onLoad('Quantities', function(){
                        $('.stockForVirtualProduct').hide();
                    });
```

145

```
                        // Line to be modified
                                $('a[id*="Combinations"]').hide();
                                $('a[id*="Shipping"]').hide();

                                tabs_manager.onLoad('Informations', function(){
                                        $('#condition').attr('disabled', true);
                                        $('#condition option[value=refurbished]').
                                        removeAttr('selected');
                                        $('#condition option[value=used]').
                                        removeAttr('selected');
                                });
                        }
                }
                else
                {
                        // 3rd case : product_type is PTYPE_SIMPLE (0)
                        $('a[id*="Combinations"]').show();
                        $('a[id*="Shipping"]').show();
                        $('#condition').removeAttr('disabled');
                        $('#condition option[value=new]').removeAttr('selected');
                        $('.stockForVirtualProduct').show();
                }
                // this handle the save button displays and warnings
                handleSaveButtons();
        });
};
```

We added a comment above the *else if* statement that needs to be modified. Naturally it is the one with the product_type == product_type_virtual condition. In its body, we'll find the line that needs to be edited as shown in Listing 4-20.

Listing 4-20. Line to Be Edited in switchProductType Function

```
$('a[id*="Combinations"]').hide();
```

Because we want the Combinations to be visible for virtual products, we switch the hide() method to show(), as shown in Listing 4-21.

Listing 4-21. Line Edited in switchProductType Function

```
$('a[id*="Combinations"]').show();
```

If we now try to create a new product in PS Back Office and select the Virtual Product option, we'll see that the Combinations tab is enabled (Figure 4-9).

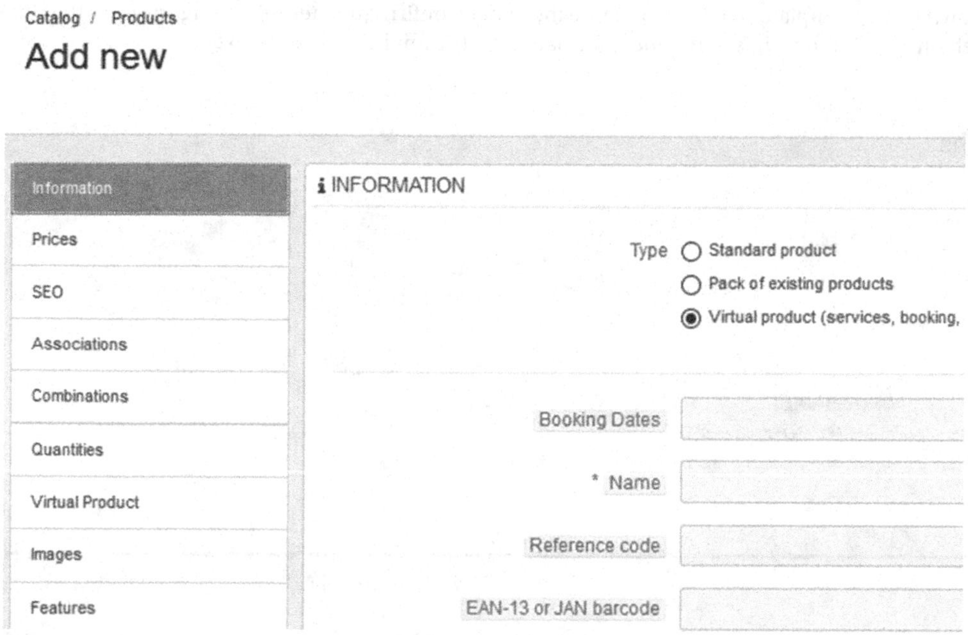

Catalog / Products

Add new

Figure 4-9. *Virtual product with Combinations tab enabled*

In this recipe, we edited `.tpl`, `.js`, and `.php` files to solve our problem and we can now manipulate combinations on virtual products.

■ **Note**   Sometimes we present the entire body of functions seeking to provide readers with an easy way of searching for the code that needs editing. Thus, the goal of this approach is to facilitate the resolution of the problem proposed.

4-6. Sending Order Confirmation Message to Various Recipients

Problem

You want to send Order Confirmation e-mails, which are received by customers after purchasing on your PS website, to different recipients.

Solution

If you want to receive notifications on your e-mail inbox regarding new orders executed on your PS website, you have different alternatives. First, you can install the Mail Alerts module, which is free. This module can be configured to dispatch notifications triggered by certain events to various e-mail addresses; one of these notifications is triggered when a new order is made on the website.

It uses is own e-mail template so if you configure the Order Confirmation template (Figure 4-10) that PS includes by default, you could be missing some information on the final message received.

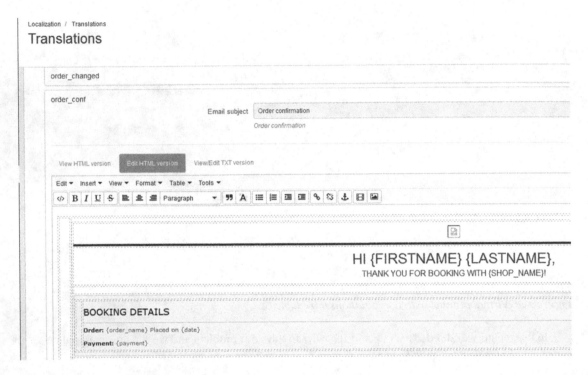

Figure 4-10. *Order Confirmation e-mail template in PS Back Office*

The other alternative is to send the PS default Order Confirmation e-mail template to the customer and other recipients (you) by editing the `classes/PaymentModule.php` file.

How It Works

As always, the recommendation is to override the `PaymentModule.php` file by copying it in `override/classes`.

This file contains the `PaymentModule` class of which most payment modules inherit. There we'll find the `validateOrder()` method with the signature shown in Listing 4-22.

Listing 4-22. validateOrder() Method Signature

```
public function validateOrder($id_cart, $id_order_state, $amount_paid, $payment_method =
'Unknown', $message = null, $extra_vars = array(), $currency_special = null, $dont_touch_
amount = false, $secure_key = false, Shop $shop = null)
```

This is the method in charge of validating orders on databases and sending confirmation e-mails. Therefore, it's the method that we need to edit in order to add extra recipients to the Order Confirmation e-mail.

Around line 777, we should find the code in Listing 4-23.

Listing 4-23. Code around Line 777 in validateOrder() Method

```
if (Validate::isEmail($this->context->customer->email)) {
            Mail::Send((int)$order->id_lang,
'order_conf',
                    Mail::l('Order confirmation', (int)$order->id_lang),
                $data,
                $this->context->customer->email,
                 $this->context->customer->firstname.' '.$this->context->
                 customer->lastname,
                null,
                null,
$file_attachement,
                null, _PS_MAIL_DIR_, false, (int)$order->id_shop
    );
```

Validate is a PS class that can be found in the classes folder and incorporates, as the name suggests, different static methods for validating e-mails, names, images attributes, an so on. The isEmail() method validates whether a given e-mail is actually valid.

The Mail class, which can be also found in the classes folder, is intended to work as the mail object used by PrestaShop. It includes one singular static method, Send(). Its signature is shown in Listing 4-24.

Listing 4-24. Send() Function on Mail.php File

```
public static function Send($id_lang, $template, $subject, $template_vars, $to,
$to_name = null, $from = null, $from_name = null, $file_attachment = null, $mode_smtp =
null, $template_path = _PS_MAIL_DIR_, $die = false, $id_shop = null, $bcc = null, $reply_to
= null)
```

In general, the arguments are self-descriptive. If we would like to send this Order Confirmation e-mail to someone else, we just need to copy the previous code and set the fifth argument ($to) to the e-mail of our new recipient. (Listing 4-25)

Listing 4-25. New Recipient Added

```
if (Validate::isEmail($this->context->customer->email)) {
            Mail::Send((int)$order->id_lang,
                    'order_conf',
                    Mail::l('Order confirmation', (int)$order->id_lang),
                $data,
                $this->context->customer->email,
                 $this->context->customer->firstname.' '.$this->context->
                 customer->lastname,
                null,
                null,
                $file_attachement,
                null, _PS_MAIL_DIR_, false, (int)$order->id_shop
    );
if (Validate::isEmail($this->context->customer->email)) {
            Mail::Send((int)$order->id_lang,
```

```
                      'order_conf',
                        Mail::l('Order confirmation', (int)$order->id_lang),
$data,
                      'arnaldo.skywalker@gmail.com',
$this->context->customer->firstname.' '.$this->context->customer->lastname,
                      null,
                      null,
                      $file_attachement,
                      null, _PS_MAIL_DIR_, false, (int)$order->id_shop
      );
```

By changing $this->context->customer->email to the e-mail of the new recipient, we can now send him the same confirmation e-mail that customers received after purchasing on the website.

4-7. Getting a Product Price

Problem

You want to get the price of a certain product.

Solution

The product price can be obtained using the static function getPriceStatic() found in classes/Product.php.

Remember PrestaShop is based on the MVC (Model-View-Controller) design pattern so, in this case, the classes folder represents the Models, the controllers folder represents the Controllers, and everything in themes represents the Views.

Another solution is to use the method getPrice() of the Product class in Product.php. this approach would require an instance object.

How It Works

The getPriceStatic() function has the signature in Listing 4-26.

Listing 4-26. getPriceStatic() Signature

```
/**
    * Returns product price
    *
    * @param int      $id_product              Product id
    * @param bool     $usetax                  With taxes or not (optional)
    * @param int|null $id_product_attribute    Product attribute id (optional).
    *    If set to false, do not apply the combination price impact.
    *    NULL does apply the default combination price impact.
    * @param int      $decimals    Number of decimals (optional)
    * @param int|null $divisor     Useful when paying many time without fees (optional)
    * @param bool     $only_reduc  Returns only the reduction amount
    * @param bool     $usereduc    Set if the returned amount will include reduction
    * @param int      $quantity    Required for quantity discount application
                                   (default value: 1)
```

```
 * @param bool      $force_associated_tax  DEPRECATED - NOT USED Force to apply the
                                           associated tax.
 *                  Only works when the parameter $usetax is true
 * @param int|null $id_customer  Customer ID (for customer group reduction)
 * @param int|null $id_cart      Cart ID. Required when the cookie is not accessible
 *                  (e.g., inside a payment module, a cron task...)
 * @param int|null $id_address   Customer address ID. Required for price (tax included)
 *                  calculation regarding the guest localization
 * @param null     $specific_price_output If a specific price applies regarding the
                                          previous parameters,
 *          this variable is filled with the corresponding SpecificPrice object
 * @param bool     $with_ecotax  Insert ecotax in price output.
 * @param bool     $use_group_reduction
 * @param Context  $context
 * @param bool     $use_customer_price
 * @return float   Product price
 */
public static function getPriceStatic($id_product, $usetax = true, $id_product_attribute
= null, $decimals = 6, $divisor = null, $only_reduc = false, $usereduc = true, $quantity =
1, $force_associated_tax = false, $id_customer = null, $id_cart = null, $id_address = null,
&$specific_price_output = null, $with_ecotax = true, $use_group_reduction = true, Context
$context = null, $use_customer_price = true)
```

Every parameter is shown in the method details section (at the top) as @param followed by its type and description. (Listing 4-27)

Listing 4-27. Product Price Obtained on a Product with id 11 and applyingprice Reduction

```
$price = Product::getPriceStatic(
11,
            $usetax,
            $id_product_attribute,
            $decimals,
            $divisor,
            $only_reduc,
true,
            $quantity,
            $force_associated_tax,
            $id_customer,
            $id_cart,
            $id_address,
            $specific_price_output,
            $with_ecotax,
            $use_group_reduction,
            $context,
            $use_customer_price
    );
```

One interesting parameter is the bool $usereduc. It allows us to either get the product price with reductions applied or not.

The final approach is to use the instance method getPrice(), as shown in Listing 4-28.

Listing 4-28. getPrice() Signature

```
/**
    * Get product price
    * Same as static function getPriceStatic, no need to specify product id
    *
    * @param bool $tax With taxes or not (optional)
    * @param int $id_product_attribute Product attribute id (optional)
    * @param int $decimals Number of decimals (optional)
    * @param int $divisor Util when paying many time without fees (optional)
    * @return float Product price in euros
    */
    public function getPrice($tax = true, $id_product_attribute = null, $decimals = 6,
    $divisor = null, $only_reduc = false, $usereduc = true, $quantity = 1)
```

As mentioned, before being able to use this function, we require an object instance. (Listing 4-29)

Listing 4-29. Getting Price on a Product with id 11

```
// instance of a product with id = 11
$product = new Produc(11);
// get the price using taxes
$product_price = $product->getPrice(true);
```

In Listing 4-29, we obtained the instance of a product with id 11 and later got its price using the getPrice() method applying taxes. We'll see more on these functions and their parameters in the following chapters.

4-8. Getting Product Name and Quantity

Problem

You want to get a product's name and quantity.

Solution

In order to get a product name and quantity, we can use the getProductName() and getQuantity() static functions of the Product class found in the classes/Product.php file.

How It Works

The getProductName() has the signature shown in Listing 4-30.

Listing 4-30. getProductName() Signature

```
/**
    * Gets the name of a given product, in the given lang
    *
    * @since 1.5.0
    * @param int $id_product
    * @param int $id_product_attribute Optional
    * @param int $id_lang Optional
    * @return string
*/
public static function getProductName($id_product, $id_product_attribute = null, $id_lang =
null)
```

To obtain the name, we must provide the product id; that's the only mandatory parameter. The $id_product_attribute and $id_lang is an optional parameter. (Listing 4-31)

Listing 4-31. Getting Name of Product with id 13

```
// Gets product with id 13 name in the current language
$name = Product::getProductName(13);
```

In order to obtain the quantity, we use the static function getQuantity(). (Listing 4-32)

Listing 4-32. getQuantity() Signature

```
/**
    * Get available product quantities
    *
    * @param int $id_product Product id
    * @param int $id_product_attribute Product attribute id (optional)
    * @return int Available quantities
    */
public static function getQuantity($id_product, $id_product_attribute = null, $cache_is_
pack = null)
```

Listing 4-33 shows how to get quantities for a given product id.

Listing 4-33. Getting Quantities from a Product with id 13 and Combination id 2

```
// Gets quantity for the specific combination2 of a product with id 13
$quantity = Product::getQuantity(13, 2);
```

There's another function for obtaining product quantities, which is getRealQuantity(). This function considers a specific warehouse being defined as a parameter.

4-9. Getting Product Categories and Features

Problem

You want to get product categories and features.

Solution

In order to get product categories, we can use the static function getProductCategories(), which can be found in the classes/Product.php file. To get product features, we can use the static function getFrontFeaturesStatic() also from Product.php.

How It Works

The getProductCategories() function has the signature shown in Listing 4-34.

Listing 4-34. getProductCategories () Signature

```
/**
    * getProductCategories return an array of categories which this product belongs to
    *
    * @return array of categories
    */
public static function getProductCategories($id_product = '')
```

As we can see, the only parameter required is the product id. (Listing 4-35)

Listing 4-35. Getting Categories of Product with id 13

```
// Getting categories in the current language
$categories = Product::getProductCategoriesFull(13, $this->context->language->id);
```

In order to obtain features, we can use the static function getFrontFeaturesStatic (). (Listing 4-36)

Listing 4-36. getFrontFeaturesStatic () Signature

```
/*
    * Select all features for a given language
    *
    * @param $id_lang Language id
    * @return array Array with feature's data
    */
    public static function getFrontFeaturesStatic($id_lang, $id_product)
```

The code in Listing 4-37 shows how to obtain features for a given product id.

Listing 4-37. Getting Features from a Product with id 13 in the Current Language

```
// Gets featuresfor a product with id 13
$features = Product::getFrontFeaturesStatic($this->context->language->id, 13);
```

We can also obtain features and categories on an instance product using the class methods getFrontFeatures() and getCategories().

4-10. Getting Order Total

Problem

You want to get the order total.

Solution

The order total is calculated in a very important method named getOrderTotal() of the Cart class found in classes/Cart.php file.

How It Works

The getOrderTotal() function has the signature shown in Listing 4-38.

Listing 4-38. getOrderTotal() function in Cart.php

```
/**
    * This function returns the total cart amount
    *
    * Possible values for $type:
    * Cart::ONLY_PRODUCTS
    * Cart::ONLY_DISCOUNTS
    * Cart::BOTH
    * Cart::BOTH_WITHOUT_SHIPPING
    * Cart::ONLY_SHIPPING
    * Cart::ONLY_WRAPPING
    * Cart::ONLY_PRODUCTS_WITHOUT_SHIPPING
    * Cart::ONLY_PHYSICAL_PRODUCTS_WITHOUT_SHIPPING
    *
    * @param bool $withTaxes With or without taxes
    * @param int $type Total type
    * @param bool $use_cache Allow using cache of the method CartRule::getContextualValue
    * @return float Order total
    */
    public function getOrderTotal($with_taxes = true, $type = Cart::BOTH, $products = null,
    $id_carrier = null, $use_cache = true)
```

The first argument indicates whether taxes should be included in the total. The $type variable acts as a filtering mechanism where Cart::BOTH indicates shipping and wrapping costs will be included in the total. Other Cart alternatives values are self-descriptive. The $products variable indicates the list of products that belong to the order, $id_carrier indicates the carrier associated with the order, and $use_cache indicates whether to use or not the cache of the CartRule::getContextualValue method. (Listing 4-39)

Listing 4-39. Saving Order Total in a Variable

```
$total_products = $this->getOrderTotal(false, Cart::BOTH);
```

This method is used by payment modules and PS Back Office throughout the shopping process to obtain different totals depending on the value of the Cart variable. We'll see more of it in Chapter 5.

Summary

In this chapter, we examined classes and controllers in PrestaShop; the chapter recipes demonstrated how the modification of these PS core files allows us to change the Back Office and the front end. In Chapter 5, we´ll describe how to transform PS into a booking system.

CHAPTER 5

Booking System

Booking systems are very common nowadays. We usually find them on touristic websites where customers might book a car for several days, a flight from one city to another, a hotel room for a couple of nights, or any other tourism-related service.

In this type of mechanism, you can have the final payment divided into two parts: a deposit paid on the website and the remaining payment paid after customers obtain the requested service. In a booking system, you may need to check whether a given product is available from a specific date range or you may need to check whether it is available at all.

In this chapter, we'll examine various recipes that will show you how to transform your PrestaShop website into a booking system. The customizations we'll explain make use of PS capacities and, in some cases, extend them. You'll learn the following:

- How to include a deposit payment for booking products

- How to change the pattern of your links

- How to improve SEO by starting a blog related to your products and services

- How to create your own hook

- How to add a configuration link to your module

- How to create a YouTube module

- How to configure your PS site using SQL queries during module installation

- How to create a module for sending e-mail notifications after order confirmation

- How to add more information to order e-mail notifications

- How to change CSS styles through a module

Note   PrestaShop includes all the facilities for easily transforming itself into a booking system.

© Arnaldo Pérez Castaño 2017
A. P. Castaño, *PrestaShop Recipes*, DOI 10.1007/978-1-4842-2574-5_5

5-1. Include a Deposit Payment for Booking Products

Problem

Include a deposit payment for booking products and services.

Solution

In order to solve this problem, we'll use PS price reduction system, shown in Figure 5-1, to obtain a deposit payment and a second payment at the moment customers actually obtain their service or product.

Figure 5-1. *Box showing product price reduction*

When we use price reduction in PS, we visually obtain, as Figure 5-1 illustrates, two prices in the product box: a real price to be paid on the website and a second price, which is the old price not paid through the website anymore.

Logically, this is exactly what we need. It's not visually displayed the way we want, but it has all the elements required: payment on the site (booking deposit) plus another payment shown below (price for the product when it's obtained).

■ **Note**   We can have price reduction for products in PS through specific prices found in the product edit page and through cart rules found in `Price Rules->Cart Rules`.

How It Works

To create a product price reduction, we go to PS Back Office following the path `Catalog->Products` and edit a product.

In the Prices tab, we'll find a Specific Prices section, as illustrated in Figure 5-2.

Figure 5-2. *Specific Prices section in Prices tab on product edit page*

In this section, we can click the Add a new specific price button to display a panel where we can add price reductions.

A price reduction can be added for a certain combination, currency, country, customer, date availability, a given product number, and so on. The reduction can be in percentage or currency units (dollars, euros, pounds, for example) as depicted in Figure 5-3.

	For	All currencies	All countries	All groups
	Customer	All customers		
	Combination	Apply to all combinations		
	Available	from [ ] to [ ]		
	Starting at	unit 1		
	Product price	$ 20.50		
	☑	Leave base price		
	Apply a discount of	0.00 Currency Units	*The discount is applied after the tax*	

✗ Cancel new specific price

Figure 5-3. *Specific Prices section in Prices tab on product edit page*

The product price can also be changed in this section for some of the previously mentioned attributes (currency, quantity, and so on), or we can stick to the base price.

Once we add a specific price, we end up with a product box as the one we have seen on Figure 5-1. All that remains now is to change that view to make it look like we are having a deposit payment plus a second payment after the service or product has been obtained.

5-2. Changing the Product View to Display Deposit Payment

Problem

You have added a specific price for a certain product and you want to display it as a deposit payment.

Solution

In order to complete this recipe, we'll need to edit the `product.tpl` file found in your current theme to change what we see in Figure 5-4 to something that resembles a deposit payment.

Figure 5-4. *Price displayed for product with reduction or discount*

Thus, the solution would be to delete the reduction box showing "-20%" and, in general, transform this view into a deposit payment view.

How It Works

In `themes/your_theme/product.tpl` file, locate around line 268, a p HTML element with id `reduction_percent`. (Listing 5-1)

Listing 5-1. Section of product.tpl File to Be Edited

```
<p id="reduction_percent" {if !$product->specificPrice || $product->specificPrice.reduction_
type != 'percentage'} style="display:none;"{/if}>
        <span id="reduction_percent_display">
        {if $product->specificPrice &&$product->specificPrice.reduction_type ==
        'percentage'}-{$product->specificPrice.reduction*100}%{/if}
        </span>
</p>
```

The previous code should be modified into the one shown in Listing 5-2.

Listing 5-2. Modificationof product.tpl Contents

```
<p {if true || !$product->specificPrice || $product->specificPrice.reduction_type !=
'percentage'} style="display:none;"{/if}>
        <span id="reduction_percent_display">
        {if $product->specificPrice && $product->specificPrice.reduction_type ==
        'percentage'}-{$product->specificPrice.reduction*100}%{/if}
        </span>
</p>
```

We simply took away the id with all of its related styles and set a true expression in the if statement to force it to always be true and avoid displaying the p HTML element. Analogously, you can do the same with the element with id reduction_amount; Figure 5-5 illustrates the result.

Figure 5-5. *Price box without percent reduction*

Above the HTML element we just edited, locate another paragraph with class our_price_display and add the "Deposit" text at the end, as shown in Listing 5-3.

Listing 5-3. Adding Deposit Text

```
<p class="our_price_display" itemprop="offers" itemscope itemtype="http://schema.org/Offer">
        {if $product->quantity > 0}<link itemprop="availability" href="http://schema.org/
        InStock"/>{/if}
{if $priceDisplay >= 0 && $priceDisplay <= 2}
        <span id="our_price_display" itemprop="price">{convertPrice price=$productPrice}
        </span>
<!--{if $tax_enabled  && ((isset($display_tax_label) && $display_tax_label == 1) ||
!isset($display_tax_label))}
{if $priceDisplay == 1}{l s='tax excl.'}{else}{l s='tax incl.'}{/if}
{/if}-->
        <meta itemprop="priceCurrency" content="{$currency->iso_code}" />
        {hook h="displayProductPriceBlock" product=$product type="price"}
        {/if}
        Deposit
</p>
```

Now that we have everything set up regarding the deposit payment, let's modify the last price. Using the CSS Editing module that we have been using in this book, change the #old_price styles, as shown in Listing 5-4.

Listing 5-4. Styles for #old_price Paragraph\

```css
#old_price {
    padding-bottom: 15px;
    font-size: 27px;
  text-decoration: none;
    display: inline-block;
    font-family: "Open Sans",sans-serif;
    line-height: 23px;
    color: black;
}
```

The final result is shown in Figure 5-6.

Figure 5-6. *Deposit price and balance due*

In this recipe, we learned how to visually adapt the price reduction or discount system that PS incorporates to adjust it into a deposit system.

■ **Note**   You will probably have to delete the product percent discount box also from other views. You can always use the browser inspector to find the code associated to the discount box and the .tpl file where the code can be found.

5-3. Calculating the Deposit Value in the Cart

Problem

You want to calculate the deposit value to eventually display it in the Cart Summary.

Solution

In order to solve this problem, we'll need to modify the getOrderTotal() method of the important Cart class found in classes/Cart.php. Remember this is the method where the total amount to be paid is calculated; thus, it's used throughout the ordering and checkout process and by payment modules (bank wire, PayPal, Stripe, and so on.).

To start, let's open the Cart.php file and locate the getOrderTotal() method.

How It Works

At the beginning of the Cart class, you will stumble on the next variable declarations, as shown in Listing 5-5.

Listing 5-5. Constant Variable Declarations around Line 144 of Cart.php File

```
const ONLY_PRODUCTS = 1;
const ONLY_DISCOUNTS = 2;
const BOTH = 3;
const BOTH_WITHOUT_SHIPPING = 4;
const ONLY_SHIPPING = 5;
const ONLY_WRAPPING = 6;
const ONLY_PRODUCTS_WITHOUT_SHIPPING = 7;
const ONLY_PHYSICAL_PRODUCTS_WITHOUT_SHIPPING = 8;
```

These variables are used to obtain different amounts depending on different conditions. For further information, refer to Chapter 4, where we detail this method.

We'll include three constant variables to the previous ones. (Listing 5-6)

Listing 5-6. Constant Variables Added to Cart Class

```
const ONLY_PRODUCTS = 1;
    const ONLY_DISCOUNTS = 2;
    const BOTH = 3;
    const BOTH_WITHOUT_SHIPPING = 4;
    const ONLY_SHIPPING = 5;
    const ONLY_WRAPPING = 6;
    const ONLY_PRODUCTS_WITHOUT_SHIPPING = 7;
    const ONLY_PHYSICAL_PRODUCTS_WITHOUT_SHIPPING = 8;
const ONLY_DUE = 9;
const ONLY_DEPOSIT = 10;
const ONLY_DEPOSIT_DUE = 11;
```

These variables will be used in this recipe and in the next two to filter the type of order total you want.

If you only want to obtain the deposit payment, you would filter by ONLY_DEPOSIT. If you need to get the balance due, you would filter by the ONLY_DEPOSIT variable, and if you want to get them both, you activate the ONLY_DEPOSIT_DUE variable.

Now, in the first lines of the getOrderTotal() method, find the declaration of the array in Listing 5-7.

Listing 5-7. In This Array, We Add the New Constant Variables.

```
$array_type = array(
                    Cart::ONLY_PRODUCTS,
                    Cart::ONLY_DISCOUNTS,
                    Cart::BOTH,
                    Cart::BOTH_WITHOUT_SHIPPING,
                    Cart::ONLY_SHIPPING,
                    Cart::ONLY_WRAPPING,
                    Cart::ONLY_PRODUCTS_WITHOUT_SHIPPING,
                    Cart::ONLY_PHYSICAL_PRODUCTS_WITHOUT_SHIPPING,
```

```
                Cart::ONLY_DEPOSIT,
                Cart::ONLY_DUE,
                Cart::ONLY_DEPOSIT_DUE,
            );
```

To be able to get our deposit payment, we need to edit the next loop, which is part of the getOrderTotal() method, as illustrated in Listing 5-8.

Listing 5-8. For Each Loop Inside, getOrderTotal() Method in Cart Class

```
foreach ($products as $product) {
        // products refer to the cart details

        if ($virtual_context->shop->id != $product['id_shop']) {
            $virtual_context->shop = new Shop((int)$product['id_shop']);
        }

        if ($ps_tax_address_type == 'id_address_invoice') {
            $id_address = (int)$this->id_address_invoice;
        } else {
            $id_address = (int)$product['id_address_delivery'];
        } // Get delivery address of the product from the cart
        if (!$address_factory->addressExists($id_address)) {
            $id_address = null;
        }

                    // The $null variable below is not used,
        // but it is necessary to pass it to getProductPrice because
        // it expects a reference.
        $null = null;
        $price = $price_calculator->getProductPrice(
            (int)$product['id_product'],
            $with_taxes,
            (int)$product['id_product_attribute'],
            6,
            null,
            false,
            true,
            $product['cart_quantity'],
            false,
            (int)$this->id_customer ? (int)$this->id_customer : null,
            (int)$this->id,
            $id_address,
            $null,
            $ps_use_ecotax,
            true,
            $virtual_context
        );

        $address = $address_factory->findOrCreate($id_address, true);
```

```
if ($with_taxes) {
        $id_tax_rules_group = Product::getIdTaxRulesGroupByIdProduct((int)$product['
        id_product'], $virtual_context);
        $tax_calculator = TaxManagerFactory::getManager($address, $id_tax_rules_
        group)->getTaxCalculator();
    } else {
        $id_tax_rules_group = 0;
    }

    if (in_array($ps_round_type, array(Order::ROUND_ITEM, Order::ROUND_LINE))) {
        if (!isset($products_total[$id_tax_rules_group])) {
            $products_total[$id_tax_rules_group] = 0;
        }
    } elseif (!isset($products_total[$id_tax_rules_group.'_'.$id_address])) {
        $products_total[$id_tax_rules_group.'_'.$id_address] = 0;
    }

    switch ($ps_round_type) {
        case Order::ROUND_TOTAL:
            $products_total[$id_tax_rules_group.'_'.$id_address] += $price *
            (int)$product['cart_quantity'];
            break;

        case Order::ROUND_LINE:
            $product_price = $price * $product['cart_quantity'];
            $products_total[$id_tax_rules_group] += Tools::ps_round($product_price,
            $compute_precision);
            break;

        case Order::ROUND_ITEM:
        default:
            $product_price = /*$with_taxes ? $tax_calculator->addTaxes($price) :
            */$price;
            $products_total[$id_tax_rules_group] += Tools::ps_round($product_price,
            $compute_precision) * (int)$product['cart_quantity'];
            break;
    }
}
```

In the previous loop, each product in the Cart is processed and its price acquired for the order total. It is in this code fragment where we need to insert the logic for calculating the deposit and balance due payments. In the case that concerns this recipe, the deposit, we will do nothing. Remember that in consistency with our philosophy, the reduced price matches the deposit and that's exactly what the getOrderTotal() method will return.

5-4. Calculating the Balance Due Value in the Cart

Problem

You want to calculate the balance due value to eventually display it in the Cart Summary.

Solution

To obtain the balance due, we'll edit the getOrderTotal() method presented in the last recipe. Specifically, we'll edit the foreach statement shown in Listing 5-8.

How It Works

Right before the code shown in Listing 5-8, in the getOrderTotal() method of the Cart class create a new variable $balance_due and initialize it to 0. Then edit the foreach as shown in Listing 5-9.

Listing 5-9. Foreach Statement in getOrderTotal() Method Modified to Calculate Balance Due Value

```
// Balance Due
            $balance_due = 0;

    foreach ($products as $product) {
        // products refer to the cart details

        if ($virtual_context->shop->id != $product['id_shop']) {
            $virtual_context->shop = new Shop((int)$product['id_shop']);
        }

        if ($ps_tax_address_type == 'id_address_invoice') {
            $id_address = (int)$this->id_address_invoice;
        } else {
            $id_address = (int)$product['id_address_delivery'];
        } // Get delivery address of the product from the cart
        if (!$address_factory->addressExists($id_address)) {
            $id_address = null;
        }

                // The $null variable below is not used,
        // but it is necessary to pass it to getProductPrice because
        // it expects a reference.
        $null = null;
        $price = $price_calculator->getProductPrice(
            (int)$product['id_product'],
            $with_taxes,
            (int)$product['id_product_attribute'],
            6,
            null,
            false,
            true,
            $product['cart_quantity'],
            false,
            (int)$this->id_customer ? (int)$this->id_customer : null,
            (int)$this->id,
            $id_address,
            $null,
            $ps_use_ecotax,
            true,
```

```
            $virtual_context
    );

                // Balance Due per product
                $balance_due_product = $price_calculator->getProductPrice(
    (int)$product['id_product'],
    $with_taxes,
    (int)$product['id_product_attribute'],
    6,
    null,
    false,
    false,
    $product['cart_quantity'],
    false,
    (int)$this->id_customer ? (int)$this->id_customer : null,
    (int)$this->id,
    $id_address,
    $null,
    $ps_use_ecotax,
    true,
    $virtual_context
    );

                // Get product price
                $balance_due_product *= $product['cart_quantity'];
                $balance_due += $balance_due_product;

                $address = $address_factory->findOrCreate($id_address, true);

    if ($with_taxes) {
        $id_tax_rules_group = Product::getIdTaxRulesGroupByIdProduct((int)$product
        ['id_product'], $virtual_context);
        $tax_calculator = TaxManagerFactory::getManager($address, $id_tax_rules_
        group)->getTaxCalculator();
    } else {
        $id_tax_rules_group = 0;
    }

    if (in_array($ps_round_type, array(Order::ROUND_ITEM, Order::ROUND_LINE))) {
        if (!isset($products_total[$id_tax_rules_group])) {
            $products_total[$id_tax_rules_group] = 0;
        }
    } elseif (!isset($products_total[$id_tax_rules_group.'_'.$id_address])) {
        $products_total[$id_tax_rules_group.'_'.$id_address] = 0;
    }

    switch ($ps_round_type) {
        case Order::ROUND_TOTAL:
            $products_total[$id_tax_rules_group.'_'.$id_address] += $price *
            (int)$product['cart_quantity'];
            break;
```

```
                case Order::ROUND_LINE:
                    $product_price = $price * $product['cart_quantity'];
                    $products_total[$id_tax_rules_group] += Tools::ps_round($product_price,
                    $compute_precision);
                    break;

                case Order::ROUND_ITEM:
                default:
                    $product_price = /*$with_taxes ? $tax_calculator->addTaxes($price) :
                    */$price;
                    $products_total[$id_tax_rules_group] += Tools::ps_round($product_price,
                    $compute_precision) * (int)$product['cart_quantity'];
                    break;
            }
        }
```

Let's examine the new lines added to the foreach statement in Listing 5-10.

Listing 5-10. Balance Due Obtained Using getProductPrice() Function

```
// Balance Due per product
                    $balance_due_product = $price_calculator->getProductPrice(
                (int)$product['id_product'],
                $with_taxes,
                (int)$product['id_product_attribute'],
                6,
                null,
                false,
                false,
                $product['cart_quantity'],
                false,
                (int)$this->id_customer ? (int)$this->id_customer : null,
                (int)$this->id,
                $id_address,
                $null,
                $ps_use_ecotax,
                true,
                $virtual_context
            );
```

First, we obtain the balance due value calling the getProductPrice() function passing false as value of the seventh argument (usereduc), that is, to get the price without discount or reduction so we will end up exactly with the balance due according to the philosophy of our booking system, which relies on product specific prices and PS discount system. (Listing 5-11)

Listing 5-11. Accumulating Balance Due Total for Each Product in Cart in $balance_due Variable

```
$balance_due_product *= $product['cart_quantity'];
$balance_due += $balance_due_product;
```

After obtaining the balance due of a product added to the cart, we multiply it by the quantity ordered; that will give us the total balance due of a product. For each product, sum that value to the $balance_due variable and in the end we'll have the total balance due.

Almost at the end of the getOrderTotal() method and to return the balance due total, we should have the code shown in Listing 5-12.

Listing 5-12. Returning Balance Due

```
if ($type == Cart::ONLY_DUE) {
        return Tools::ps_round((float)$balance_due, $compute_precision);
}

return Tools::ps_round((float)$order_total, $compute_precision);
```

In the next recipe, we'll describe the last modification required in the getOrderTotal() method.

5-5. Obtaining Deposit Payment Plus Balance Due

Problem

You want to obtain the value that represents the deposit payment plus the balance due of these products in our booking system.

Solution

In order to solve this problem, we'll add another modification to the getOrderTotal() method of the Cart class.

How It Works

We'll use the Cart::ONLY_DEPOSIT_DUE variable for filtering and returning the deposit plus balance due whenever that constant is submitted as argument of the getOrderTotal() method.

The modification would be in the end of the method, as shown in Listing 5-13.

Listing 5-13. Returning Balance Due Plus Deposit Value

```
if ($type == Cart::ONLY_DUE_DEPOSIT) {
            return Tools::ps_round((float)$balance_due + (float)$order_total,
            $compute_precision);
            }

            return Tools::ps_round((float)$order_total, $compute_precision);
}
```

Now that we have everything settled in the Cart class we can start analyzing in the following recipes how to display this new information we just added in the Cart Summary.

5-6. Getting Deposit and Balance Due Values into Cart Summary

Problem

You want to add the deposit and balance due values into the Cart Summary.

Solution

To solve this problem, we'll edit the `classes/Cart.php` file and more specifically the `getSummaryDetails()` method.

How It Works

In the `getSummaryDetails()` method, all Smarty variables used in the Cart Summary are calculated. The first lines of the method are shown in Listing 5-14.

Listing 5-14. First Lines of getSummaryDetails() Method

```php
public function getSummaryDetails($id_lang = null, $refresh = false)
        {
                $context = Context::getContext();
                if (!$id_lang)
                        $id_lang = $context->language->id;

                $delivery = new Address((int)$this->id_address_delivery);
                $invoice = new Address((int)$this->id_address_invoice);

                // New layout system with personalization fields
                $formatted_addresses = array(
                        'delivery' => AddressFormat::getFormattedLayoutData($delivery),
                        'invoice' => AddressFormat::getFormattedLayoutData($invoice)
                );

                $base_total_tax_inc = $this->getOrderTotal(true);
                $base_total_tax_exc = $this->getOrderTotal(false);

$total_tax = $base_total_tax_inc - $base_total_tax_exc;
```

We'll change the value associated with the $base_total_tax_inc and $base_total_tax_exc variables in Listing 5-15.

Listing 5-15. New Balues for $base_total_tax_inc and $base_total_tax_exc Variables

```php
$base_total_tax_inc = $this->getOrderTotal(true, Cart::ONLY_DEPOSIT_DUE);
$base_total_tax_exc = $this->getOrderTotal(false);
```

The $base_total_tax_inc variable represents the total price of the product or service (deposit + balance due). If you want to avoid having any tax involved, you can comment the $total_tax = $base_total_tax_inc - $base_total_tax_exc line and set $total_tax to 0.

Now locate the $summary array declaration and edit it as shown in Listing 5-16 to add the total_due and total_deposit Smarty variables.

Listing 5-16. Smarty Variables for Cart Summary

```
$summary = array(
            'delivery' => $delivery,
            'delivery_state' => State::getNameById($delivery->id_state),
            'invoice' => $invoice,
            'invoice_state' => State::getNameById($invoice->id_state),
            'formattedAddresses' => $formatted_addresses,
            'products' => array_values($products),
            'gift_products' => $gift_products,
            'discounts' => array_values($cart_rules),
            'is_virtual_cart' => (int)$this->isVirtualCart(),
            'total_discounts' => $total_discounts,
            'total_discounts_tax_exc' => $total_discounts_tax_exc,
            'total_wrapping'=> $this->getOrderTotal(true, Cart::ONLY_WRAPPING),
            'total_wrapping_tax_exc' => $this->getOrderTotal(false, Cart::ONLY_WRAPPING),
            'total_shipping' => $total_shipping,
            'total_shipping_tax_exc' => $total_shipping_tax_exc,
            'total_products_wt' => $total_products_wt,
            'total_products' => $total_products,
            'total_price' => $base_total_tax_inc,
            'total_tax' => $total_tax,
            'total_price_without_tax' => $base_total_tax_exc,
            'is_multi_address_delivery' => $this->isMultiAddressDelivery() || ((int)
Tools::getValue('multi-shipping') == 1),
            'free_ship' =>!$total_shipping && !count($this->getDeliveryAddressesWithoutCarri
ers(true, $errors)),
            'carrier' => new Carrier($this->id_carrier, $id_lang),
                'total_due' => $this->getOrderTotal(true, Cart::ONLY_DUE),
                'total_deposit' => $this->getOrderTotal(true, Cart::ONLY_DEPOSIT)
        );
```

Once we complete this recipe, we'll have the Smarty variables declared in Listing 5-16 available from every template file related to the Cart Summary.

5-7. Displaying Deposit Payment and Balance Due in the Cart Summary

Problem

You want to display the deposit payment and balance due in the Cart Summary.

Solution

In Recipe 5-6, we were able to associate the deposit payment and balance due values with Smarty variables that are submitted to the Cart Summary template files; now we just need to find a place in the .tpl files to put those variables.

How It Works

In your current theme folder, locate the shopping-cart.tpl file; this is the file where the table representing the Cart Summary is created. We'll edit it to incorporate the deposit and balance due payments.

Modify the first 50 lines of shopping-cart.tpl to make it look like a reservations summary, as shown in Listing 5-17.

Listing 5-17. Modifying Cart Summary Text into Reservations Summary Text

```
{capture name=path}{l s='Your Reservations'}{/capture}

<h1 id="cart_title" class="page-heading">{l s='Reservations summary'}
        {if !isset($empty) && !$PS_CATALOG_MODE}
                <span class="heading-counter">{l s='You have reserved:'}
                        <span id="summary_products_quantity">{$productNumber} {if
                        $productNumber == 1}{l s='product'}{else}{l s='products'}{/if}</span>
                </span>
        {/if}
</h1>

{if isset($account_created)}
        <p class="alert alert-success">
                {l s='Your account has been created.'}
        </p>
{/if}

{assign var='current_step' value='summary'}
{include file="$tpl_dir./order-steps.tpl"}
{include file="$tpl_dir./errors.tpl"}

{if isset($empty)}
        <p class="alert alert-warning">{l s='You have no reservations.'}</p>
{elseif $PS_CATALOG_MODE}
        <p class="alert alert-warning">{l s='This site has not accepted your new order.'}</
p>
{else}
```

Now locate a table HTML element with id cart_summary and edit its <thead> tag content so it includes Deposit and Balance Due columns, as shown in Listing 5-18.

Listing 5-18. Adding Balance Due and Deposit Columns in Reservations Summary

```
<table id="cart_summary" class="table table-bordered {if $PS_STOCK_MANAGEMENT}stock-
management-on{else}stock-management-off{/if}">
        <thead>
                <tr>
                <th class="cart_product first_item">{l s='Tour/Car'}</th>
                <th class="cart_description item">{l s='Description'}</th>
                        {if $PS_STOCK_MANAGEMENT}
                        {assign var='col_span_subtotal' value='3'}
                        <th class="cart_avail item text-center">{l s='Availability'}</th>
                        {else}
```

```
                    {assign var='col_span_subtotal' value='2'}
                    {/if}
            <th class="cart_unit item text-right">{l s='Balance Due'}</th>
            <th class="cart_unit item text-right">{l s='Reservation Deposit'}</th>
            <th class="cart_quantity item text-center">{l s='Qty'}</th>
            <th class="cart_delete last_item"> </th>
            <th class="cart_total item text-right">{l s='Total'}</th>
            </tr>
        </thead>
```

Next, we'll modify the last part of the tfoot tag of the cart-summary table to add rows in the Reservations Summary for detailing balance due and deposit payments, as shown in Listing 5-19.

Listing 5-19. Adding Total Balance Due and Total Deposit Rows in Reservations Summary

```
{* Deposit Due *}
                <tr class="cart_total_price">
                <td colspan="{$col_span_subtotal}" class="total_price_container text-right">
                    Total Deposit
                </td>
                <td colspan="2" class="price">
        <span id="total_deposit">{displayPrice price=$total_deposit}</span>
                </td>
        </tr>
        {* Balance Due *}
        <tr class="cart_total_price">
        <td colspan="{$col_span_subtotal}" class="total_price_container text-right">
                Total Due
        </td>
        <td colspan="2" class="price">
                <span id="total_due">{displayPrice price=$total_due}</span>
        </td>
</tr>
        <tr class="cart_total_price">
                <td colspan="{$col_span_subtotal}" class="total_price_container text-right">
                <span>{l s='Total'}</span>
<div class="hookDisplayProductPriceBlock-price">
{hook h="displayCartTotalPriceLabel"}
</div>
        </td>
                                        {if $use_taxes}
                                                <td colspan="2" class="price" id="total_
                                                price_container">
                <span id="total_price">{displayPrice price=$total_price}</span>
                                                </td>
                                        {else}
                        <td colspan="2" class="price" id="total_price_container">
                                                <span id="total_price">{displayPrice
                                                price=$total_price_without_tax}</span>
                                                </td>
                                        {/if}
                        </tr>
                </tfoot>
```

In order to add the balance due value per product, we must edit the shopping-cart-product-line.tpl file; this is where all rows describing products in the Cart Summary are generated. (Listing 5-20)

Listing 5-20. First Lines of shopping-cart-product-line.tpl File Where Balance Due Has Been Added to Product Row

```
<tr id="product_{$product.id_product}_{$product.id_product_attribute}_{if $quantityDisplayed
> 0}nocustom{else}0{/if}_{$product.id_address_delivery|intval}{if !empty($product.
gift)}_gift{/if}" class="cart_item{if isset($productLast) && $productLast &&
(!isset($ignoreProductLast) || !$ignoreProductLast)} last_item{/if}{if isset($productFirst)
&& $productFirst} first_item{/if}{if isset($customizedDatas.$productId.$productAttrib
uteId) AND $quantityDisplayed == 0} alternate_item{/if} address_{$product.id_address_
delivery|intval} {if $odd}odd{else}even{/if}">
        <td class="cart_product">
                <a href="{$link->getProductLink($product.id_product, $product.link_rewrite,
                $product.category, null, null, $product.id_shop, $product.id_product_
                attribute, false, false, true)|escape:'html':'UTF-8'}"><img src="{$link-
                >getImageLink($product.link_rewrite, $product.id_image, 'small_default')
                |escape:'html':'UTF-8'}" alt="{$product.name|escape:'html':'UTF-8'}"
                {if isset($smallSize)}width="{$smallSize.width}" height="{$smallSize.
                height}" {/if} /></a>
        </td>
        <td class="cart_description">
                {capture name=sep} : {/capture}
                {capture}{l s=' : '}{/capture}
                <p class="product-name"><a href="{$link->getProductLink($product.id_product,
                $product.link_rewrite, $product.category, null, null, $product.id_shop,
                $product.id_product_attribute, false, false, true)|escape:'html':'UTF-
                8'}">{$product.name|escape:'html':'UTF-8'}</a></p>
                        {if $product.reference}<small class="cart_ref">{l s='SKU'}{$smarty.
                        capture.default}{$product.reference|escape:'html':'UTF-8'}</small>{/if}
                {if isset($product.attributes) && $product.attributes}<small><a
                href="{$link->getProductLink($product.id_product, $product.link_
                rewrite, $product.category, null, null, $product.id_shop, $product.
                id_product_attribute, false, false, true)|escape:'html':'UTF-
                8'}">{$product.attributes|@replace: $smarty.capture.sep:$smarty.capture.
                default|escape:'html':'UTF-8'}</a></small>{/if}
        </td>
        {if $PS_STOCK_MANAGEMENT}
                <td class="cart_avail"><span class="label{if $product.quantity_available
                <= 0 && isset($product.allow_oosp) && !$product.allow_oosp} label-danger{elseif
                $product.quantity_available <= 0} label-warning{else} label-success{/if}">
                {if $product.quantity_available <= 0}{if isset($product.allow_oosp) &&
                $product.allow_oosp}{if isset($product.available_later) && $product.available_
                later}{$product.available_later}{else}{l s='In Stock'}{/if}{else}{l s='Out of
                stock'}{/if}{else}{if isset($product.available_now) && $product.available_now}
                {$product.available_now}{else}{l s='In Stock'}{/if}{/if}</span>{if !$product.
                is_virtual}{hook h="displayProductDeliveryTime" product=$product}{/if}</td>
        {/if}
        <td class="balance-due text-right">{displayPrice price=$product.price_without_
        specific_price}</td>
```

Notice that we are taking the price without specific price or reduction as the balance due. That fits perfectly with the booking system approach followed throughout this chapter; the final result can be seen in Figure 5-7.

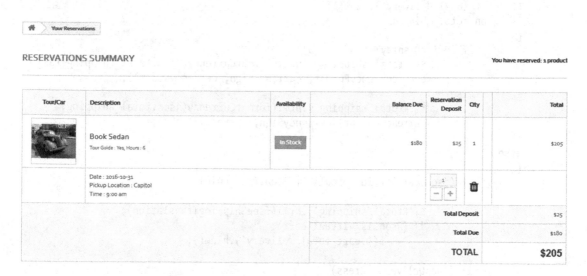

Figure 5-7. *Deposit and balance due values displayed in Reservations Summary*

We are almost done, but there's a point we haven't covered yet: the AJAX component in the Cart Summary. When you click the minus and plus signs next to the delete button, all values (deposit, balance due, total) should be updated. This is accomplished through AJAX calls.

To synchronize the AJAX calls with the changes we have made, we'll need to edit the your_theme/js/cart-summary.js file. Open it and find the updateCartSummary() function.

Within its body, around line 962, we'll modify the final lines of the function to set the values for the balance due and deposit payments, as shown in Listing 5-21.

Listing 5-21. Setting Values for Deposit and Balance Due Payments in cart-summary.js file

```
// Cart summary
        $('#summary_products_quantity').html(nbrProducts + ' ' + (nbrProducts > 1 ?
        txtProducts : txtProduct));
        if (priceDisplayMethod !== 0)
                $('#total_product').html(formatCurrency(json.total_products, currencyFormat,
                currencySign, currencyBlank));
        else
                $('#total_product').html(formatCurrency(json.total_products_wt,
                currencyFormat, currencySign, currencyBlank));
        $('#total_price').html(formatCurrency(json.total_price, currencyFormat,
        currencySign, currencyBlank));
        $('#total_due').html(formatCurrency(json.total_due, currencyFormat, currencySign,
        currencyBlank));
        $('#total_deposit').html(formatCurrency(json.total_deposit, currencyFormat,
        currencySign, currencyBlank));
        $('#total_price_without_tax').html(formatCurrency(json.total_price_without_tax,
        currencyFormat, currencySign, currencyBlank));
```

```
$('#total_tax').html(formatCurrency(json.total_tax, currencyFormat, currencySign,
currencyBlank));

$('.cart_total_delivery').show();
if (json.total_shipping > 0)
{
        if (priceDisplayMethod !== 0)
                $('#total_shipping').html(formatCurrency(json.total_shipping_tax_
                exc, currencyFormat, currencySign, currencyBlank));
        else
                $('#total_shipping').html(formatCurrency(json.total_shipping,
                currencyFormat, currencySign, currencyBlank));
}
else
{
        if (json.carrier.id != null || json.free_ship)
        {
                $('#total_shipping').html(freeShippingTranslation);
                if (json.is_virtual_cart)
                        $('.cart_total_delivery').hide();
        }
        if (!hasDeliveryAddress)
                $('.cart_total_delivery').hide();
}

if (json.total_wrapping > 0)
{
        $('#total_wrapping').html(formatCurrency(json.total_wrapping,
        currencyFormat, currencySign, currencyBlank));
        $('#total_wrapping').parent().show();
}
else
{
        $('#total_wrapping').html(formatCurrency(json.total_wrapping,
        currencyFormat, currencySign, currencyBlank));
        $('#total_wrapping').parent().hide();
}
}
```

Now when we add or remove products from the cart, we'll see that the deposit and balance due values are updated correctly.

5-8. Detailing Balance Due in Order Confirmation E-mail

Problem

You want to detail the balance due value in Order Confirmation e-mails.

Solution

In order to solve this problem, we'll edit the PaymentModule class contained in the file of the same name, classes/PaymentModule.php.

How It Works

Open the PaymentModule.php file and locate the validateOrder() method. Around line 383, add the line shown in Listing 5-22.

Listing 5-22. Line Added to validateOrder() Method

```
$balance_due = $this->context->cart->getOrderTotal(false, Cart::ONLY_DUE);
```

Now, find the $data array and add at the beginning the $balance_due variable, as shown in Listing 5-23.

Listing 5-23. Balance Due Value Added to $data Array

```
$data = array(
                        '{firstname}' => $this->context->customer->firstname,
                                        '{balance_due}' => $balance_due,
'{lastname}' => $this->context->customer->lastname,
                        '{email}' => $this->context->customer->email,
                        '{delivery_block_txt}' => $this->_getFormatedAddress($delivery, "\n"),
                        '{invoice_block_txt}' => $this->_getFormatedAddress($invoice, "\n"),
                        '{delivery_block_html}' => $this->_getFormatedAddress($delivery,
                        '<br />', array(
                            'firstname'    => '<span style="font-weight:bold;">%s</span>',
                            'lastname'     => '<span style="font-weight:bold;">%s</span>'
                        )),
```

To conclude, we visit PS Back Office and go to Localization->Translations and then select Type of Translation as "Email templates translations," theme as your_theme, and language as the current language of your store. Select the order_conf template and edit it (Figure 5-8).

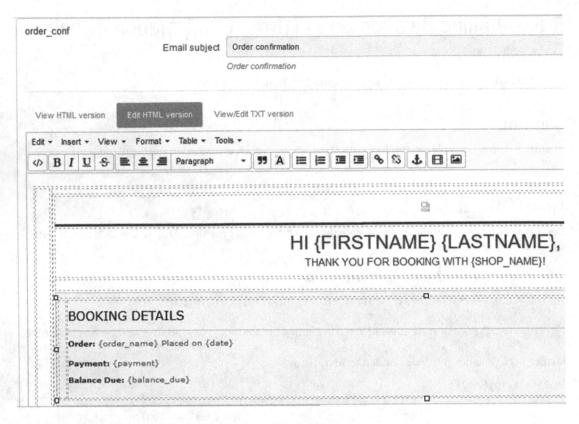

Figure 5-8. *Balance due added to Order Confirmation e-mail*

The modification can be seen in Figure 5-8. We simply added a Balance Due text followed by the variable and we added to the `$data` array of the `validateOrder()` method in `PaymentModule.php` file. You may feel free to detail the balance due anywhere you want in the `order_conf` template; the value will be displayed in the confirmation e-mail.

Summary

In this chapter, we examined several recipes that illustrated how PrestaShop can be transformed into a booking system. In Chapter 5, we'll demonstrate how it can be transformed into an events-based system.

CHAPTER 6

■ ■ ■

Events-Based System

In Chapter 5, we described how to transform PrestaShop into a booking system. In this chapter, we'll demonstrate how we can transform PS into an events-based system. As we did in Chapter 5, we'll use the very own features that PS offers to carry out this transformation.

An event is something that occurs in time. It can be organized and scheduled, and it can involve different actors that can be objects, living beings, and so forth. In ordinary language, we may say that an event can be a ceremony, festival, party, and so on.

In this chapter, we'll consider the creation of a scheduled event, that is, an event that will take place on a specific date, at a designated time, and at a determined location. Furthermore, people will be able to sign up for it. You will learn the following:

- How to create and associate a Date attribute for your events products

- How to sell tickets

- How to sell unlimited tickets

■ **Note**   PrestaShop is an extensive, adaptable content management system that you can intelligently customize and transform into a booking system or an events-based system. In this chapter, we will transform a common PS product into an events product.

6-1. Creating and Associating a Date Attribute for Your Events products

Problem

You want to create a Date attribute for your events products and associate it to them as combinations.

Solution

To start constructing our scheduled events product, we'll create the necessary Date attribute to allow customers to select the date they would like to be at the event. Then we will associate its values to products using combinations.

© Arnaldo Pérez Castaño 2017
A. P. Castaño, *PrestaShop Recipes*, DOI 10.1007/978-1-4842-2574-5_6

How It Works

Go to PS Back Office and then click `Catalog->Product Attributes`, as shown in Figure 6-1.

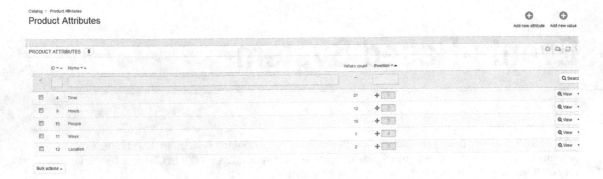

Figure 6-1. *Product attributes section*

On the upper right corner, click the Add New Attribute button and fill in the fields on the new page, putting the name you want for the new attribute; in our case, we named it Date. (Figure 6-2)

Catalog / Product Attributes

Add New Attribute

❶ ATTRIBUTES

* Name	Date
* Public name	Date
URL	

When the Layered Navigation Block m uses the attribute's name, but you can

Meta title	

When the Layered Navigation Block m PrestaShop uses the attribute's name,

Indexable	YES NO

Use this attribute in URL generated by

* Attribute type	Drop-down list ▾

Figure 6-2. *Adding Date attribute*

Once you are back on the Product Attributes page, click the Add New Value field and add the values you want for the Date attribute as dates (for example, Sun Feb 12th 2017 9pm). This is illustrated in Figure 6-3.

Catalog / Product Attributes

Add New Value

ⓘ VALUES

* Attribute group	Date ▼
* Value	Sun Feb 12th 2017 9pm
URL	
	When the Layered Navigation Block module is uses the attribute's name, but you can change
Meta title	
	When the Layered Navigation Block module is PrestaShop uses the attribute's name, but you

Figure 6-3. Adding Date attribute values as dates

After creating the Date attribute, we just need to associate its values to our events product using combinations as depicted in Figure 6-4.

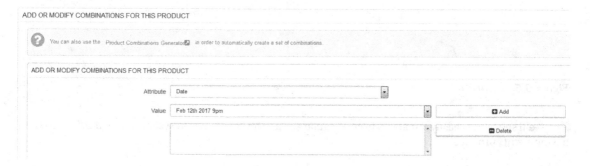

Figure 6-4. Date value added

For that purpose, we go to PS Back Office and click Catalog->Products. We select the product that we would like to have as our events product and then click the Combinations tab and delete every combination except for those having Date as attribute.

6-2. Selling Tickets

Problem

You want to sell a limited number of tickets for your event.

Solution

In Recipe 6-1, we added combinations for the different values associated with the Date attribute. Assuming we have configured PS to allow orders, even when products are out of stock and after making slight modifications in the product.tpl file (hiding Condition text and changing "Quantity" to "Tickets") of your current theme, we should end up having a product similar to the one depicted in Figure 6-5.

■ **Note** You can configure PS to allow orders by default when a product is out of stock visiting the Back Office and going to Preferences->Products.

Figure 6-5. *Event oroduct*

We'll see how to easily mutate PS from a regular shop to an events-based system giving the illusion of having events products.

How It Works

To sell a certain number of tickets, we must edit the product's quantities in PS Back Office (Figure 6-6). Go there and for each Date attribute value (combination), select the number of tickets that you would like to sell on that date.

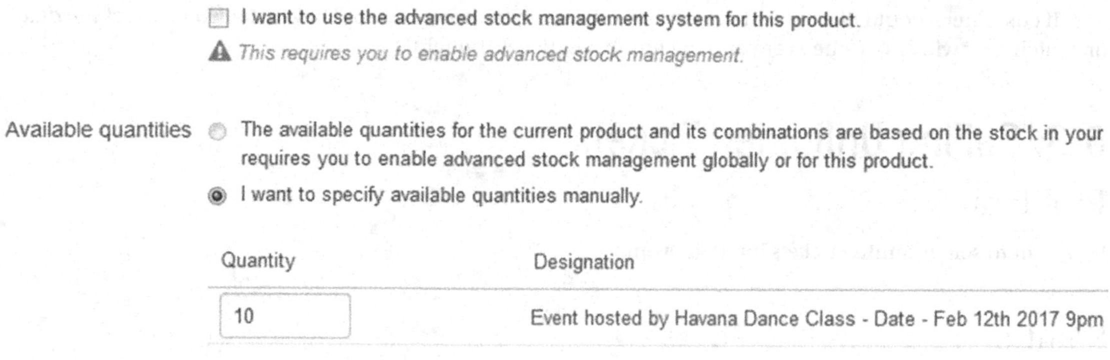

☐ I want to use the advanced stock management system for this product.

⚠ *This requires you to enable advanced stock management.*

Available quantities   ◯ The available quantities for the current product and its combinations are based on the stock in your
requires you to enable advanced stock management globally or for this product.

◉ I want to specify available quantities manually.

Quantity	Designation
10	Event hosted by Havana Dance Class - Date - Feb 12th 2017 9pm

Figure 6-6. *Defining quantity for each combination (date) in product edit page*

Also, change the Availability Settings to display the texts shown in Figure 6-7.

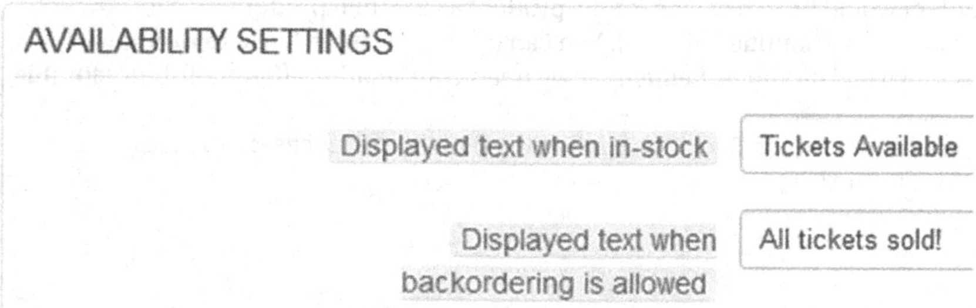

AVAILABILITY SETTINGS

Displayed text when in-stock   Tickets Available

Displayed text when   All tickets sold!
backordering is allowed

Figure 6-7. *Changing availability settings to show "Tickets Available" when a product is in stock and "All tickets sold!" in any other case*

After making these simple modifications, we'll have our events product, as we can see in Figure 6-8.

Figure 6-8. *Events product*

If customers would like to buy tickets on our site, they can easily do so. They just need to select the date on which they will attend the event and the number of tickets bought.

6-3. Selling Unlimited Tickets

Problem

You want to sell unlimited tickets for your event.

Solution

The solutions to this problem can be found in a combination of some of the recipes we have seen so far.

How It Works

The first solution to this problem would be to have the events product as a virtual product. As we know from previous recipes, that takes away quantities (tickets). You can refer to Chapter 4, where we showed how to enable combinations for virtual products. Remember we need combinations (`Date` attribute) for this product.

Another alternative would be to go to the Back Office following path `Preferences->Products` and disable the stock management. (Figure 6-9)

Figure 6-9. *Stock management disabled*

Once we have no stock management, quantities on the product page will become a useless tab, as shown in Figure 6-10.

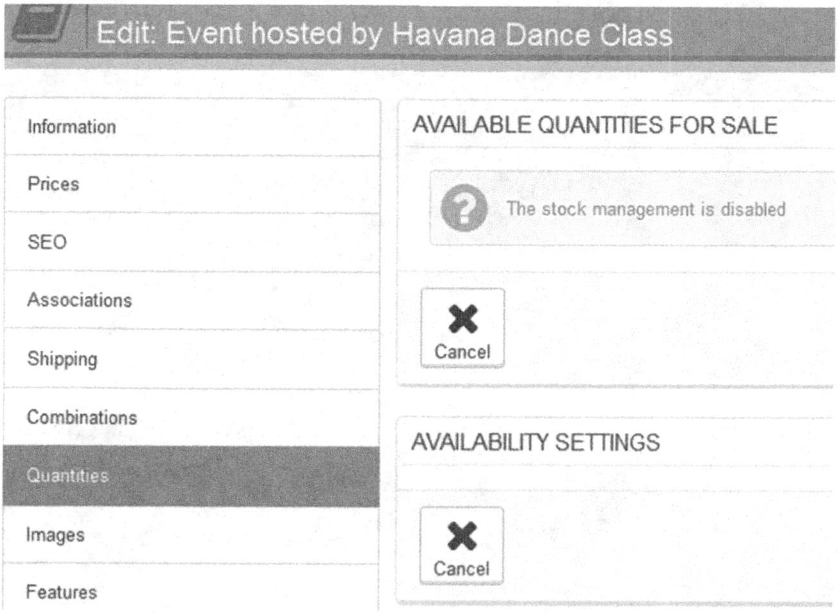

Figure 6-10. Quantities tab in product page after disabling stock management

After making these modifications, we'll see that we can sell as many tickets as we want for any date.

Summary

Throughout this chapter we examined, in just a few recipes, how we can easily turn PS into an events-based system. In Chapter 7, we will present various recipes that will give us the possibility of improving our Search Engine Optimization (SEO).

CHAPTER 7

■ ■ ■

SEO

Once you have completed the installation, configuration, and customization of your PrestaShop website, you can have the most amazing e-commerce business ever created. However, all the time, work, and effort put into this project could be in vain if people are not aware of your existence. Remember the Web is a gigantic network of servers and websites, and it is difficult to stand out in such a huge nest. Thus, a typical phase that precedes any revenue you could obtain from your online business is the marketing phase.

Search Engine Optimization (SEO) is a marketing discipline and a common practice in the e-commerce world today. It is represented as a set of techniques that looks for positioning a website high in the result pages of different search engines when people query them under certain terms and keywords. In general, SEO relates to the programming, design, and content of your website. When it is improved, it should increase your site's traffic. Words on your web pages as well as external links pointing to your site are all aspects to be considered in your SEO strategy.

In this chapter, we'll be examining various recipes for improving your SEO in PrestaShop. Some of these recipes represent general strategies and not only apply to PS, but to any website. You will learn the following:

- How to activate friendly URLs in PS

- How to change the pattern of your links

- How to improve SEO by starting a blog related to your products and services

- How to define SEO for your categories in PS

- How to define SEO for your products in PS

- How to generate `robots.txt` file

- How to link to social networks

- How to speed up PS to improve your SEO

- How to improve your SEO by having a responsive theme

- How to select the appropriate domain name

- How to generate the sitemap of your PS

- How to increase the number of links pointing at your website

---

■ **Note** Choosing profitable and niche keywords is vital in SEO. You can use tools such as Google Adwords (keyword planner) to discover how popular or searched the keywords you intend to include in your website actually are.

© Arnaldo Pérez Castaño 2017
A. P. Castaño, *PrestaShop Recipes*, DOI 10.1007/978-1-4842-2574-5_7

7-1. How to Activate Friendly URLs in PS

Problem

You want to have friendly, pretty URLs on your PS site.

Solution

To set up the Friendly URLs option, we visit the Back Office and go to `Preferences-> SEO & URLs` and then to the SET UP URLS section. We switch the Friendly URL field to "Yes," as shown in Figure 7-1.

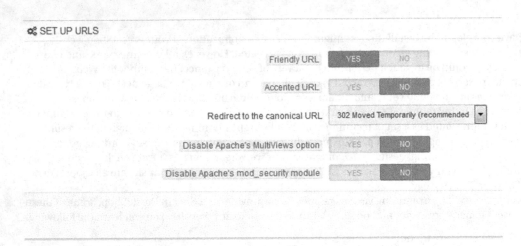

Figure 7-1. *Activating Friendly URLs*

The rest of the fields represent configuration issues that will allow you to define several details regarding your friendly URLs.

■ **Note**   Non-friendly URLs are full of `GET` variables and are difficult to read (for example, `www.havanaclassiccartour.com/index.php?id_product=30&controller=product`). On the other hand, friendly URLs are easy to read and remember (`www.havanaclassiccartour.com/classic-convertibles/30-book-classic-convertible.html`).

How It Works

To understand what actions and advantages we can take when activating friendly URLs in PrestaShop, let's inspect the `Preferences-> SEO&URLs` page.

We start by examining the SEO and URLs section (Figure 7-2), where we can define the title of each page and its friendly URL.

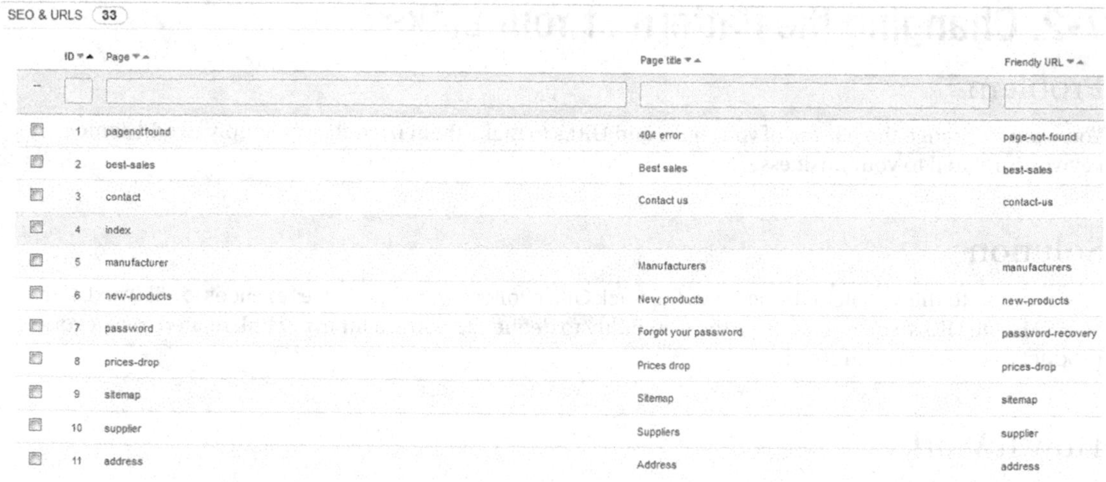

Figure 7-2. *SEO & URLs section*

Usually our index page has no page title or friendly URL defined; however, it's very important to define one for it. The index page should identify your business and it's normally where the majority of business keywords can be found. Therefore, having a title assigned to it as well as some meta keywords and a meta description is a good idea. Click the Edit button next to it; the resulting page should be similar to the one shown in Figure 7-3. We'll edit it.

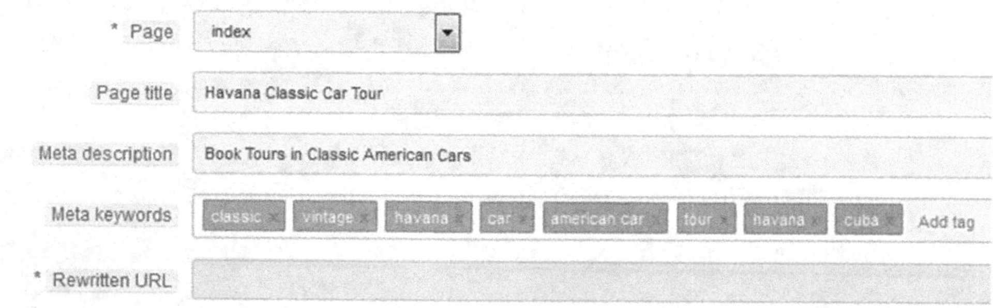

Figure 7-3. *Editing Index page*

In the SET UP URLs section where we activated the Friendly URLs option, we should also define the Canonical URL to "301 Moved Permanently." Search engines tend to penalize duplicated content in your website. Thus, if you have both http://havanaclassiccartour.com and www.havanaclassiccartour.com, they are interpreted as different websites with the same content. Canonical URLs prevent duplication issues by making one and the other URL seem like the same.

■ **Note** Today more and more websites try to show friendly URLs to ease the indexing process. In non-friendly URLs, search engines do not add the proper weight to the correct words; thus, a diminishing of the page content value and ranking usually occurs.

7-2. Changing the Pattern of Your Links

Problem

You want to change the pattern of your links and URLs to make them friendlier or simply to add some keywords related to your business.

Solution

The solution to this problem lies again in the Back Office following the path Preferences-> SEO&URLs. In the SCHEMA OF URLs' section, we have the possibility to define the pattern for every link related to categories, products, cms pages, and so on.

How It Works

To change a pattern, we need to consider the set of keywords required by each type of link, as can be seen in Figure 7-4.

Figure 7-4. *Defining URLS patterns*

In the categories route, for instance, we have the following definition: {id}-{rewrite}. This indicates that the category URL will have its id displayed followed by a hyphen and its name, as depicted in Figure 7-5. This should be defined in its SEO title; we'll shortly see where to define it.

Figure 7-5. URL seen in the browser

We can find available keywords for each category route below its text field (Figure 7-6). Let's change the category route by adding the meta_title keyword and clicking the Save button at the bottom of the section.

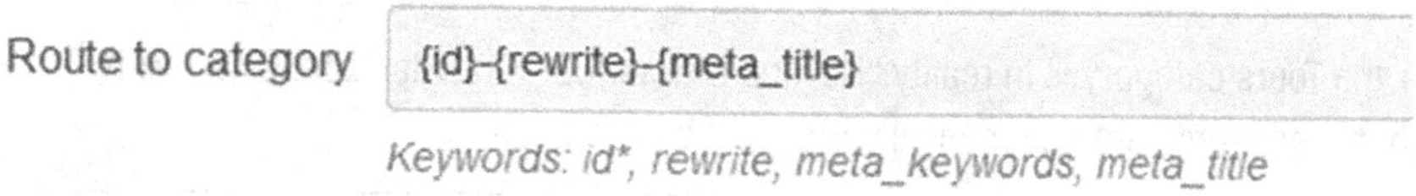

Route to category   {id}-{rewrite}-{meta_title}

                Keywords: id*, rewrite, meta_keywords, meta_title

Figure 7-6. Route to category after adding the meta_title keyword

We can see the change in our URL as illustrated in Figure 7-7.

Figure 7-7. URL for Tours category after changing the pattern

Even though the id keyword must be present on the URL, we can select the location where we want to put it. For instance, we might decide to put it at the end of the URL, as can be seen in Figure 7-8.

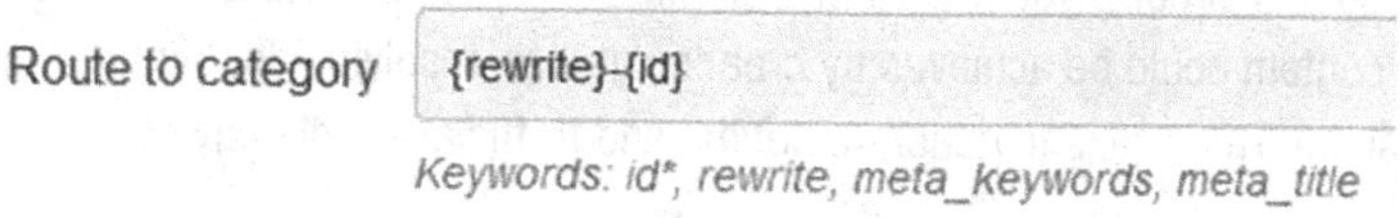

Route to category   {rewrite}-{id}

                Keywords: id*, rewrite, meta_keywords, meta_title

Figure 7-8. Putting id at the end of the URL

Once we have saved our new change and reloaded any category page, the modification should be visible (Figure 7-9).

Figure 7-9. URL with id at the end

In this manner, you can freely change your URLs to make them friendlier and also to add keywords that might serve your interests.

■ **Note**   The meta_title for the Tours category is in reality "Havana Classic Car Tour, Malecon, Cigar, Mob, Hemingway Tours." Spaces between words are automatically replaced by a hyphen.

7-3. Improving SEO by Starting a Blog Related to Your Products and Services

Problem

You want to improve your SEO by adding high-quality content on a blog related to your products or services.

Solution

Content is "the king" in the world of marketing and SEO. For search engines, content represents everything on a web page: links, body content, images, meta tags, and so on. Most e-commerce websites focus on offering products and services, but sometimes forget to provide useful and well-written content. Search engines actually love fresh content; content generated on a regular basis makes them see activity, and that goes in favor of your site's rank.

■ **Note**   In a blog, you don't sell your products directly; you sell them indirectly by producing valuable content that gets people interested. This valuable content could be achieved by creating guides, resolving doubts, answering questions, providing tips, and so on. The idea is to generate debate and traffic and indirectly get people to the store.

How It Works

Creating a blog on PrestaShop depends basically on your hosting service. What you would do in PS is simply create a link in the top menu to your blog's domain.

To add a blog link to our top menu, we go to Modules and Services and search the Top Horizontal Menu module (Figure 7-10).

Figure 7-10. Top horizontal menu

In the module's configuration page, we simply need to go to the ADD A NEW LINK section and add a new link named Blog. Its link would be your blog's URL, as illustrated in Figure 7-11.

Figure 7-11. Adding new link to horizontal menu

Once added, you simply need to put the new link in the desired position with the rest of the links in the top menu.

■ **Note** The blog you create could be a WordPress blog. Most hosting services provide an easy installation to this popular CMS. You just need to install it on a subdomain; if your domain is havanaclassiccartour.com, then your blog's domain could be blog.havanaclassiccartour.com.

7-4. Defining SEO for Your Categories in PS

Problem

You want to define meta_title and meta_description for your categories to improve your SEO.

Solution

To define SEO features for our categories, we first need to access the category we want to configure. In the PS Back Office, go to Catalog-> Categories and click the category that you want to edit (Figure 7-12).

Figure 7-12. Categories page

How It Works

In our case, we are editing the Tours category, so once you access the edit page, look for every field with the "Meta" prefix. You should find three right away: "Meta title," "Meta description," and "Meta keywords" (Figure 7-13).

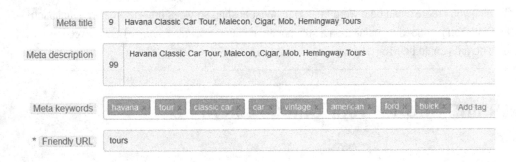

Figure 7-13. Editing category page

In the Meta fields, you should write something that describes your product or service category, always respecting the number of characters imposed. The Friendly URL field defines the URL to be used for the category if Friendly URL is activated in your PS site.

■ **Note** Remember the Meta Title, Meta Description, and Meta Keywords field can be used in your URLs when defining their schema under `Preferences-> SEO&URLs`.

7-5. Defining SEO for Your Products in PS

Problem

You want to define meta_title and meta_description for your products to improve your SEO.

Solution

To access the SEO tab of our products, we go to the Back Office and follow the path `Catalog->Products` and then click Edit on the product in which we want to define SEO features. Finally, we click SEO on the left panel in the product edit page.

How It Works

In the SEO tab, we'll find three fields: Meta title, Meta description, and Friendly URL, as shown in Figure 7-14.

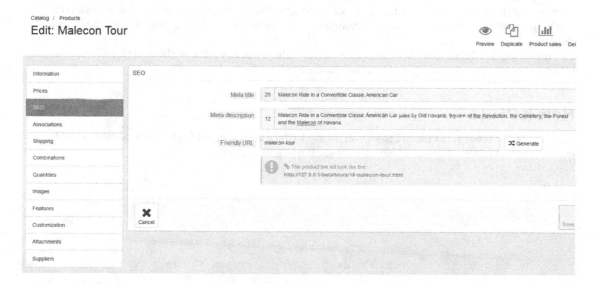

Figure 7-14. *Product edit page*

In the Meta title field for a product, the first keywords we write should be the ones we try to position, the ones that appropriately represent our business. Also, the text we put there shouldn't be similar to the product's category title.

The description is usually an extension of the title, and it should be attractive to customers and include the keywords we want people and search engines to read. Again, we can't go beyond the character limit for each field, so we must be direct and concise in every text.

The Friendly URL field allows you to define the URL that will be used for this product if you have activated the Friendly URL option in the Back Office.

> ■ **Note**   The meta description text is the one that appears on the Google Search results page right below your shop's link. It's important to keep in mind that we must provide original content for both the Meta title and Meta description fields. If we copy their texts from some external source, we could be adding duplicating content to our website, and search engines do not appreciate duplicated content.

7-6. Generating robots.txt File

Problem

You want to generate the `robots.txt` file for your PS site.

Solution

The Robot Exclusion Protocol, represented by the `robots.txt` file, is a method for avoiding the inclusion of information you want or think should be private on search results. The `robots.txt` file will act as a request mechanism, asking certain robots to not pay attention to specific files and directories of your site during their search.

Including this file in your PS package root can be useful if you have directories and files whose content might not properly classify the purpose or intention of your business.

How It Works

To generate the `robots.txt` file in PS, we visit the Back Office and go to `Preferences-> SEO&URLs`. At the end, we'll see the ROBOTS FILE GENERATION section (Figure 7-15).

Figure 7-15. *Robots file generation section*

When we click the Generate robots txt file button, a new file will be generating at the root of our PS package. In case we already have one there, it will be overwritten.

The first 30 lines of the file will look like the lines shown in Figure 7-16.

```
1   # robots.txt automaticaly generated by PrestaShop e-commerce open-source solution
2   # http://www.prestashop.com - http://www.prestashop.com/forums
3   # This file is to prevent the crawling and indexing of certain parts
4   # of your site by web crawlers and spiders run by sites like Yahoo!
5   # and Google. By telling these "robots" where not to go on your site,
6   # you save bandwidth and server resources.
7   # For more information about the robots.txt standard, see:
8   # http://www.robotstxt.org/robotstxt.html
9   User-agent: *
10  # Allow Directives
11  Allow: */modules/*.css
12  Allow: */modules/*.js
13  # Private pages
14  Disallow: /*?orderby=
15  Disallow: /*?orderway=
16  Disallow: /*?tag=
17  Disallow: /*?id_currency=
18  Disallow: /*?search_query=
19  Disallow: /*?back=
20  Disallow: /*?n=
21  Disallow: /*&orderby=
22  Disallow: /*&orderway=
23  Disallow: /*&tag=
24  Disallow: /*&id_currency=
25  Disallow: /*&search_query=
26  Disallow: /*&back=
27  Disallow: /*&n=
28  Disallow: /*controller=addresses
29  Disallow: /*controller=address
30  Disallow: /*controller=authentication
31  Disallow: /*controller=cart
```

Figure 7-16. *Robots file*

Every line preceded by a "#" character is a comment and will not have any effect when processed. The User-agent line defines the robots for which the rules below apply. The "*" character indicates "All." As a result, in the previous case the rules will apply for every robot that visits your PS site.

The Allow and Disallow directives indicate the files that can be accessed and the ones that are private or prohibited. The Disallow /*?orderby= directive, for example, specifies that no robot can access an URL that includes ?orderby=. Remember the "*" applies for everything, so the directive would prohibit all of the following:

/products?orderby=name,/categories?orderby=name, etc.

In the robots.txt file, you could have different rules for various robots:

    User-agent: MyBot

    Disallow:

    User-agent: *

    Disallow: /

In the last example, we are allowing a robot named MyBot to search through our entire website. Any other robot will not be allowed to search our website.

■ **Note** The directives `User-agent: *` combined with `Disallow: /` would be applied to every robot, prohibiting access to every file stored in the root folder.

7-7. Linking to Social Networks

Problem

You want to have your PS site linked to different social networks accounts that you created for your business.

Solution

Social media is one of the most successful ways for getting people to know about the products and services that you offer at your store. Not all social networks will be practical for your products or services, so you must always select those that are appropriate and create a unique strategy for each (remember search engines don't appreciate duplicated content).

By default, links to social accounts in PrestaShop can be found at the footer (Figure 7-17).

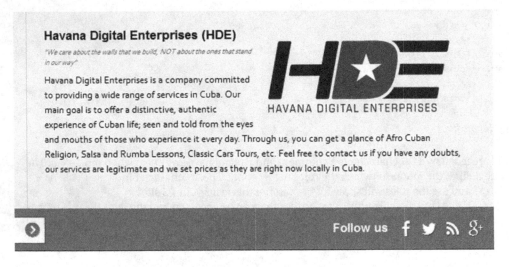

Figure 7-17. Social network links in the footer

These links can be customized in PS and their configuration can be achieved in the Back Office following the path Modules and Services-> Theme Configurator, as illustrated in Figure 7-18.

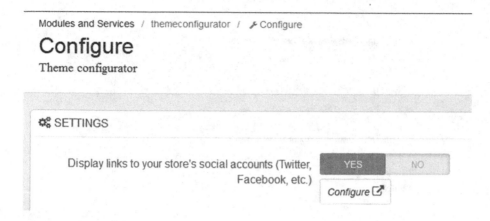

Figure 7-18. *Theme Configurator module*

Locate a text named "Display links to your store's social accounts (Twitter, Facebook, etc.)," and make sure the switch is set to Yes. Then click the Configure button below.

How It Works

Once we click the Configure button, we'll find a list of social networks that PS includes by default (Figure 7-19).

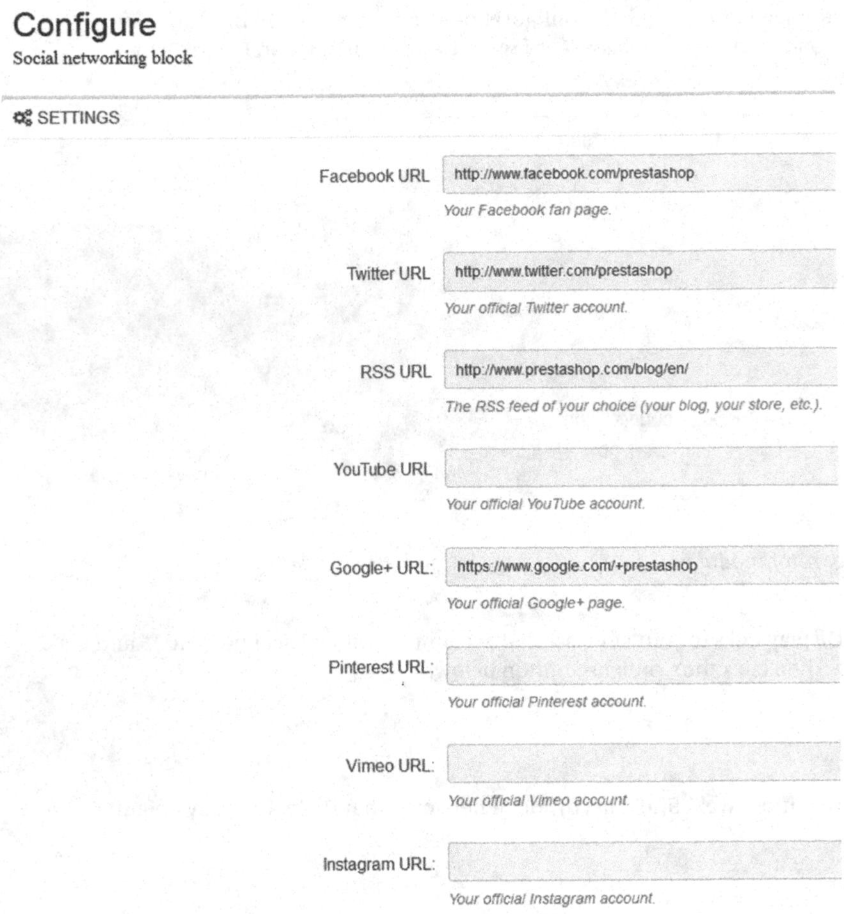

Configure

Social networking block

⚙ SETTINGS

Facebook URL	http://www.facebook.com/prestashop

Your Facebook fan page.

Twitter URL	http://www.twitter.com/prestashop

Your official Twitter account.

RSS URL	http://www.prestashop.com/blog/en/

The RSS feed of your choice (your blog, your store, etc.).

YouTube URL	

Your official YouTube account.

Google+ URL:	https://www.google.com/+prestashop

Your official Google+ page.

Pinterest URL:	

Your official Pinterest account.

Vimeo URL:	

Your official Vimeo account.

Instagram URL:	

Your official Instagram account.

Figure 7-19. *Social networks links*

Finally, you can go one text field at a time when setting URLs for your social networks. In case you don't have an account or don't wish to show it in the row of social networks links in the footer, simply leave that field empty as we can see that occurs with Vimeo, Pinterest, or Instagram in the previous example.

■ **Note** There's a shorter way to configure your social network links in the Back Office. Find the Social Networking Block module and click the Configure button; it will take you to the same page we saw at the end of this recipe, where we can define an URL for each social network.

7-8. Speeding Up PS to Improve SEO

Problem

You want to speed up your PS site to improve your SEO.

Solution

A very important feature when positioning your website is its page-loading speed. Fast-load page is not only good for SEO as it delivers a positive customer experience, but it also increases the chances of obtaining revenue. PS incorporates various performance improvements that we can take advantage of in order to obtain a higher page loading speed.

How It Works

In the Back Office, we go to Advanced Parameters->Performance. In the Smarty section, we switch the Cache option to Yes and we set Template Compilation to Never recompile template files, as shown in Figure 7-20.

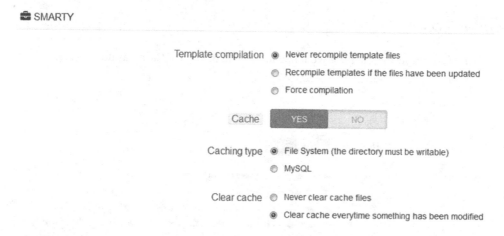

Figure 7-20. *Activating cache for Smarty*

In the CCC (Combine, Compress, and Cache) section (Figure 7-21), switch every option to Yes; this should significantly decrease the loading time of your page.

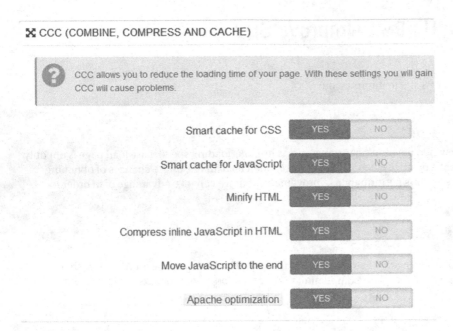

✖ CCC (COMBINE, COMPRESS AND CACHE)

CCC allows you to reduce the loading time of your page. With these settings you will gain
CCC will cause problems.

Smart cache for CSS	YES / NO
Smart cache for JavaScript	YES / NO
Minify HTML	YES / NO
Compress inline JavaScript in HTML	YES / NO
Move JavaScript to the end	YES / NO
Apache optimization	YES / NO

Figure 7-21. *Activating CCC*

Finally, go to the end, locate the Caching section, and activate the Use of Cache as depicted in
Figure 7-22.

⬜ CACHING

Use cache | YES / NO

Caching system
- ⦿ File System (the directory must be writable)
- ⦾ Memcached via PHP::Memcache (you must install the Memcache PECL extension)
- ⦾ Memcached via PHP::Memcached (you must install the Memcached PECL extension)
- ⦾ APC (you must install the APC PECL extension)
- ⦾ Xcache (you must install the Xcache extension)

Directory depth | 1

Figure 7-22. *Activating cache*

After having activated these options, you should start to notice that your website loads pages a lot faster.
The main reason behind this accelerated speed is the cache.

A web cache mechanism consists in temporarily saving processed files (.css, .js, images, and so on) in
memory (hard disk) so the next time they are required, their loading process can be completed easily and in
less time.

7-9. Improving Your SEO by Having a Responsive Theme

Problem

You want to improve your SEO.

Solution

Starting in PS 1.5, the default theme is responsive so there's nothing to do there. If you are using PS < 1.5, you should try to find a responsive theme. Google likes it when your website adapts correctly to all devices, dimensions, and users.

How It Works

If you need to select a new responsive theme, visit the Back Office and go to Preferences-> Themes (Figure 7-23).

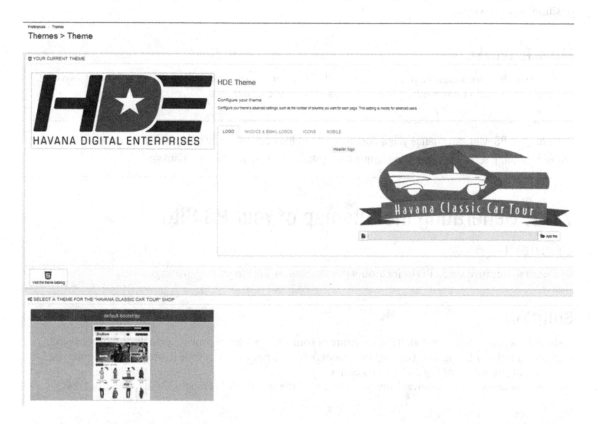

Figure 7-23. *Theme selector page*

There you can select your theme and also define your icons, favicon and logos for invoices and e-mails.

> ■ **Note** You can check whether your PS theme is responsive from your PC simply by using features incorporated in web browsers today. In Mozilla Firefox, for instance, you can activate the Responsive Design View on the Developer tab. This will allow you to see how your website will looks at different resolutions.

7-10. Selecting the Appropriate Domain Name

Problem

You want to improve your SEO.

Solution

The domain name you select can help you achieve a higher ranking and it should contain some of your most relevant keywords. This strategy is important as it's one of the key factors that Google considers when positioning your website.

How It Works

If you are in the cars business, you probably would like your domain name to include car-related keywords somewhere. It could be something like www.havanaclassiccartour.com.

> ■ **Note** In PS, you can change yours domain name in the Back Office by going to Preferences-> SEO&URLs. When migrating, you usually need to change the domain's name through the database.

7-11. Generating the Sitemap of Your PS Site

Problem

You want to improve your SEO by including the sitemap.xml file in your PS package root.

Solution

A sitemap is a file where you detail the structure of your site, seeking to provide Google and other search engines with this information. Google bots (robots), for example, read this file in order to trace your site in a more intelligent way, making their access easier.

To generate your sitemap.xml file, you can install the free module Google Sitemap (Figure 7-24).

Figure 7-24. Google Sitemap module

Once you have installed it, click the Configure link to start configuring it, as shown in Figure 7-25.

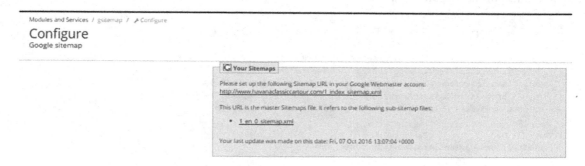

Figure 7-25. Google sitemap configuration page

How It Works

For your `sitemap.xml` file to be linked to Google, you need to create a Google Webmaster account and set the URL to the file.

You also have the possibility of configuring your sitemap indicating the pages to be included and the update frequency of your store, as illustrated in Figure 7-26.

Configure your Sitemap

Several Sitemaps files will be generated depending on how your server is configured and on the number of activated products in your catalog.

How often do you update your store?

weekly

Check this box if you wish to check the presence of the image files on the server ☑

check all ☐

Indicate the pages that you do not want to include in your Sitemaps file:

- ☐ Address [address]
- ☐ Best sales [best-sales]
- ☑ Discount [discount]
- ☑ Identity [identity]
- ☑ [module-bankwire-payment]
- ☐ My account [my-account]
- ☐ Order confirmation [order-confirmation]
- ☐ Forgot your password [password]
- ☐ Search [search]
- ☑ Suppliers [supplier]

- ☐ Addresses [addresses]
- ☐ Cart [cart]
- ☐ Guest tracking [guest-tracking]
- ☐ Havana Classic Car Tour [index]
- ☑ [module-bankwire-validation]
- ☑ New products [new-products]
- ☐ Order follow [order-follow]
- ☐ Credit slip [order-slip]
- ☐ Prices drop [prices-drop]
- ☐ Sitemap [sitemap]

- ☐ Login [authentication]
- ☐ Contact us [contact]
- ☑ Order history [history]
- ☑ Manufacturers [manufacturer]
- ☑ [module-cronjobs-callback]
- ☐ Order [order]
- ☐ Order [order-opc]
- ☐ 404 error [pagenotfound]
- ☐ Products Comparison [products-comparison]
- ☑ Stores [stores]

Generate Sitemap   This can take several minutes

Figure 7-26. Configuring sitemap

Finally, you also have the option to automatically generate your sitemap by setting up a Cron task on your hosting provider (Figure 7-27).

```
<?xml version="1.0" encoding="UTF-8"?>
<urlset
      xmlns="http://www.sitemaps.org/schemas/sitemap/0.9"
      xmlns:xsi="http://www.w3.org/2001/XMLSchema-instance"
      xsi:schemaLocation="http://www.sitemaps.org/schemas/sitemap/0.9
             http://www.sitemaps.org/schemas/sitemap/0.9/sitemap.xsd">
<!-- created with Free Online Sitemap Generator www.xml-sitemaps.com -->

<url>
  <loc>http://www.havanaclassiccartour.com/</loc>
</url>
<url>
  <loc>http://www.havanaclassiccartour.com/contact-us</loc>
</url>
<url>
  <loc>http://www.havanaclassiccartour.com/4-about-us</loc>
</url>
<url>
  <loc>http://www.havanaclassiccartour.com/8-gallery</loc>
</url>
<url>
  <loc>http://www.havanaclassiccartour.com/7-classic-sedan</loc>
</url>
<url>
  <loc>http://www.havanaclassiccartour.com/9-classic-convertible</loc>
</url>
<url>
  <loc>http://www.havanaclassiccartour.com/tours-15</loc>
</url>
<url>
  <loc>http://www.havanaclassiccartour.com/classic-convertibles/30-book-c
</url>
<url>
  <loc>http://www.havanaclassiccartour.com/classic-convertibles/41-book-c
</url>
```

Figure 7-27. *Sitemap.xml file*

By having an XML file, you can use your sitemap to provide meta data to Google about certain content types included in your website (image, videos, and so on.).

7-12. Increasing the Number of Links Pointing at Your WebSite

Problem

You want to improve your SEO by increasing the number of links pointing at your website.

Solution

Google uses a family of ranking algorithms known as Page Rank; these algorithms assign a relevance number to each document indexed by a search engine. The higher our page rank is, the higher we'll be in the results page.

Taking advantage of the algorithm's insight, we can improve our ranking by trying to increase the number of external links that point to our website.

Registering your URL on free web directories is usually a good practice. It creates external links pointing at your site, and a positive result should be perceived in the long run.

How It Works

The common strategy to boost your page rank is to increase the number of links that point toward your website. The higher the number of websites referring to it, the higher your page rank should get.

Google considers not only the volume of links that point to you, but also the quality of those links. The quality of a link equals the page rank of the site that contains the link to your site. The more popular the site, the higher the contribution it will provide to your ranking.

For instance, let us assume that our site havanaclassiccartour.com, which is a startup, has a low ranking and we are trying to improve it. Somehow we create links to our website on tripadvisor.com and lonelyplanet.com. Since both sites are very popular and definitely have a higher page rank than ours, they will boost our page rank and eventually move us higher in the results page (Figure 7-28).

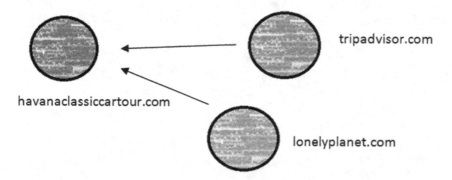

Figure 7-28. *Page rank situation—important pages make you important*

Furthermore, creating partnerships with different stores and online businesses to create links pointing to our website, products, and services will also contribute positively in improving our ranking.

Summary

In this chapter, we presented different recipes that will help us improve our SEO. Chapter 8 will convey a simple but useful topic that must be applied when extensions or customizations are required; we are referring to maintenance.

CHAPTER 8

■ ■ ■

Maintenance

During the development, customization, or extension phase of your PrestaShop website, you may have the need to create new products or complete modifications to some of your already published products.

In this chapter, we'll examine various recipes that will show you how to appropriately modify your site or provide maintenance. You will learn the following:

- How to set PS in maintenance mode

- How to edit the text displayed in maintenance mode

- How to edit the image displayed in maintenance mode

■ **Note** Whenever you need to edit your PS website, you should enter maintenance mode and leave part of your shop inaccessible.

8-1. Set PS in Maintenance Mode

Problem

You want to set PrestaShop in maintenance mode.

Solution

In order to solve this problem, we'll visit PS Back Office and then go to `Preferences->Maintenance`, as shown in Figure 8-1.

© Arnaldo Pérez Castaño 2017
A. P. Castaño, *PrestaShop Recipes*, DOI 10.1007/978-1-4842-2574-5_8

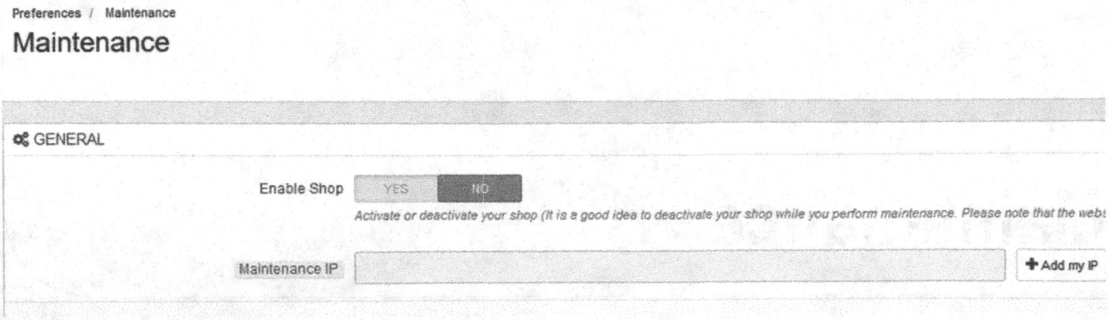

Preferences / Maintenance

Maintenance

⚙ GENERAL

Enable Shop   YES   NO

Activate or deactivate your shop (It is a good idea to deactivate your shop while you perform maintenance. Please note that the web

Maintenance IP   [   ]   **+ Add my IP**

Figure 8-1. *Maintenance page*

The page is very simple. It merely contains an Enable Shop switch button, a Maintenance IP text field, and an Add my IP button.

How It Works

To activate maintenance mode in our store, we must enable it by switching the Enable Shop button to "No" on the Maintenance page. Once disabled, we can click the Add my IP button to allow our IP address to access the site. Alternatively, we can add as many address as we want, all separated by commas in the Maintenance IP text field (Figure 8-2).

Figure 8-2. *Maintenance page*

After clicking the Save button on the lower right corner, we can visit our website and verify, as depicted in Figure 8-3, that the maintenance mode has been indeed activated.

Figure 8-3. *Maintenance template displayed when accessing your website*

Notice the image is out of the central box. In the next recipes, we'll demonstrate how to edit, adjust, and modify the maintenance template displayed in Figure 8-3.

8-2. Edit the Text Displayed in Maintenance Mode

Problem

You want to edit the maintenance template and show a different text.

Solution

To solve this problem, we must look for the maintenance template file following path `themes/your_theme/maintenance.tpl`.

How It Works

Open the `maintenance.tpl` file and let's edit it; its code is extremely simple (Listing 8-1).

Listing 8-1. Code of maintenance.tpl File

```
<!DOCTYPE html>
<html lang="{$language_code|escape:'html':'UTF-8'}">
<head>
        <meta charset="utf-8">
        <title>{$meta_title|escape:'html':'UTF-8'}</title>
{if isset($meta_description)}
        <meta name="description" content="{$meta_description|escape:'html':'UTF-8'}">
```

```
{/if}
{if isset($meta_keywords)}
        <meta name="keywords" content="{$meta_keywords|escape:'html':'UTF-8'}">
{/if}
        <meta name="robots" content="{if isset($nobots)}no{/if}index,follow">
        <link rel="shortcut icon" href="{$favicon_url}">
<link href="{$css_dir}maintenance.css" rel="stylesheet">
<link href='//fonts.googleapis.com/css?family=Open+Sans:600' rel='stylesheet'>
</head>
<body>
        <div class="container">
                        <div id="maintenance">
                        <div class="logo">
<img src="{$logo_url}" {if $logo_image_width}width="{$logo_image_width}"{/if} {if $logo_
image_height}height="{$logo_image_height}"{/if} alt="logo" /></div>
                        {$HOOK_MAINTENANCE}
                <div id="message">
                <h1 class="maintenance-heading">
{l s='We\'ll be back soon.'}</h1>
                        {l s='We are currently updating our shop and will be back really
                        soon.'}
                        <br />
                                {l s='Thanks for your patience.'}
                                </div>
                        </div>
                </div>
        </div>
</body>
</html>
```

In case you want to display a different text, you just need to edit the div HTML element with id "message," which is shown in Listing 8-1. Listing 8-2 shows the result.

Listing 8-2. Modification of maintenance.tpl Message

```
<div id="message">
        <h1 class="maintenance-heading">{l s='We\'ll be back soon'}</h1>
{l s='We are currently updating Havana Classic Car Tour and we will be back really soon.'}
        <br />
        {l s='Thank you!!'}
</div>
```

Now, as seen in Figure 8-4, we will be able to see the result of this modification when visiting the website in maintenance mode.

We'll be back soon

We are currently updating Havana Classic Car Tour and we
will be back really soon.
Thank you!!

Figure 8-4. *New text on maintenance.tpl file*

In the next recipe, we'll find out how to change the image shown on the maintenance page.

8-3. Edit the Image Displayed in Maintenance Mode

Problem

You want to edit the maintenance template and resize or change the image displayed.

Solution

In order to solve this problem, once again we will edit the `themes/your_theme/maintenance.tpl` file.

How It Works

Going back to the maintenance image shown in Figure 8-3, we can see that it was not properly centered and its size exceeded the frame of the box in which it was contained. We will resize it now to make it fit the box that contains it. Find the following div HTML element in the `maintenance.tpl` file shown in Listing 8-3.

Listing 8-3. Fragment of maintenance.tpl File Where img HTML Element Is Declared

```
<div class="logo">
          <img src="{$logo_url}" {if $logo_image_width}width="{$logo_image_width}"{/if}
          {if $logo_image_height}height="{$logo_image_height}"{/if} alt="logo" />
</div>
```

Modify the previous code as shown in Listing 8-4.

Listing 8-4. Fragment of maintenance.tpl File Where img HTML Element Is Declared Modified

```
<div class="logo">
<img src="{$logo_url}" width="400px" height="180px" alt="logo" />
</div>
```

After completing this edit, the image should properly fit into the box and for different resolutions, as shown in Figure 8-5.

Figure 8-5. *Image resize in maintenance.tpl file*

The ideal scenario of course would be to have the width and height attributes as shown in Listing 8-5.

Listing 8-5. Width and Height Attributes of img HTML Tag

```
<img src="{$logo_url}" width="100%" height="auto" alt="logo" />
```

If you have those image properties set as shown in Listing 8-5, the image will fit properly into the box in any resolution.

Summary

In this chapter, we examined three recipes that allow us to properly handle our shop's maintenance system. Throughout this book, we have presented many recipes that provide us with easy-to-follow guides on how to customize many of the wonderful features that this powerful content management system offers.

Index

© Arnaldo Pérez Castaño 2017
A. P. Castaño, *PrestaShop Recipes*, DOI 10.1007/978-1-4842-2574-5

Get the eBook for only $4.99!

Why limit yourself?

Now you can take the weightless companion with you wherever you go and access your content on your PC, phone, tablet, or reader.

Since you've purchased this print book, we are happy to offer you the eBook for just $4.99.

Convenient and fully searchable, the PDF version enables you to easily find and copy code—or perform examples by quickly toggling between instructions and applications.

To learn more, go to http://www.apress.com/us/shop/companion or contact support@apress.com.